Law Firm Marketing Toolkit

Related titles from Law Society Publishing:

Lexcel Business Continuity Planning Toolkit
The Law Society

Lexcel Client Care Toolkit (2nd edition)
The Law Society

Lexcel Financial Management and Business Planning Toolkit
The Law Society

Lexcel Information Management Toolkit
The Law Society

Lexcel People Management Toolkit
The Law Society

Lexcel Risk Management Toolkit (2nd edition)
The Law Society

Conveyancing Quality Scheme Toolkit (2nd edition)
The Law Society

Marketing Legal Services (2nd edition)
David Monk and Alastair Moyes

All books from Law Society Publishing can be ordered through good bookshops or direct from our distributors, Prolog, by telephone 0870 850 1422 or email **lawsociety@prolog.uk.com**. Please confirm the price before ordering.

For further information or a catalogue, please contact our editorial and marketing office by e-mail **publishing@lawsociety.org.uk**.

Law Firm Marketing Toolkit

The Law Society

The Law Society

ISBN 978-1-907698-79-8

Published in 2013 by the Law Society
113 Chancery Lane, London WC2A 1PL

Typeset by Columns Design XML Ltd, Reading
Printed by TJ International Ltd, Padstow, Cornwall

The paper used for the text pages of this book is FSC® certified. FSC (the Forest Stewardship Council®) is an international network to promote responsible management of the world's forests.

FSC
www.fsc.org
MIX
Paper from
responsible sources
FSC® C013056

Contents

Foreword

I'm constantly buoyed by the innovation and enthusiasm I see from solicitors from across England and Wales. Many of our members are tackling the challenges they face with imagination, drive and determination, but at the moment everyone can do with a helping hand.

It's no good us telling our solicitors and firms to 'market' themselves better if we can't tell you how you might be able to do that.

We don't expect you to be marketing geniuses but we do hope our members recognise it is an increasingly tough market to be working in and anything solicitors or firms can do to make themselves more attractive to clients can only help. There are no magic tricks and this toolkit takes a 'how to do it' approach, but do it you must; because if you don't, your competitors will.

Our members are solicitors, not marketeers, so this toolkit is designed to give you some practical advice on how you can stand out from the crowd, attract new clients and keep them coming back for more without the big budgets of others.

Marketing is never going to be a substitute for high-quality legal work, but it can help you to present yourselves effectively in a new and more highly competitive legal services market. I hope you find it useful.

Lucy Scott-Moncrieff

President of the Law Society

May 2013

Preface

Marketing is often a misunderstood subject. When we set out to write this toolkit we wanted to demystify it, explain how the principles of good marketing can help you and provide you with some practical guidance that will allow you to market you (and your firm) effectively.

If it is not the production of legal work, or the accounting for that work, then it is marketing. Everything a firm does, in every one of its areas, affects how people think about the practice – whether they use it, whether they came back to it and, importantly, whether they recommend it.

This toolkit gives you some of the key principles you may want to consider when thinking about the customer experience – how you attract new clients, how to treat them and how you can keep your clients coming back to you rather than going to another legal service provider. This toolkit is a start, but if you are interested then you can find more detail in books such as *Marketing Legal Services* (2nd edition, Law Society, 2011) and from the Law Society Law Management Section and Small Firms Division.

The Law Society would like to thank David Monk of Marketlaw Ltd (**www.marketlaw.co.uk**), who has prepared most of the material for this toolkit.

1 Understanding the benefits your practice gives your clients

Marketing is in part about providing clients and prospects with the services they require that produce sufficient benefits to justify the price being charged, in the light of similar services being offered by the competition. These benefits must be provided from the firm's existing resources, or resources reasonably available to the firm, while ensuring that the supply of these services creates an agreed level of profit.

In trying to achieve the above we have to recognise the negative start point faced by the legal profession. No one wakes up and determines to buy some solicitor's time today. Solicitors and their services are a derived need over which we have no control, either in creating that need or influencing its timing. Solicitors cannot even create the desire to receive the benefits that they have to offer. No one wants a solicitor! They want to move house, start a business, draw up a will, get a divorce, etc. Solicitors are just a step in that process.

The task for firms therefore is to be available when the time is right and be sure that the very real benefits are presented in a way that is understood by the potential client.

Much as you may wish, your firm cannot rely on being the automatic choice of even loyal, satisfied clients. Even they are continually subjected to the promotional activity of other solicitors and especially the 'new competition'. (In later chapters we will look at methods of improving your firm's chances through client registration schemes and regular client communications.)

Firms therefore need to prepare in advance the detail of the many reasons there are to use or recommend them, as opposed to other options, before they even consider how they are going to communicate these benefits to clients or prospects and other recommenders.

What is being proposed is a full-scale benefit analysis of your firm.

The first recommendation is to involve all staff at every level. The accounts department will have a different view to that of fee earners, but one that is just as valid. Reception will hear more truth from the 'ordinary' client than any senior partner and secretarial and support staff can frequently offer really valuable insights and observations.

Annex 1C contains an indicative staff memo, outlining why the exercise is being undertaken, what it is hoped it will achieve, why the staff at all levels are being involved and an outline of what each member of staff should think about. It also suggests a timescale.

Annex 1A contains a benefits analysis return form that can be distributed to all staff members to complete. It contains questions to form an outline of the benefits of:

- *Going to a solicitor*. Remember there are more alternative providers of legal services today.
- *Going to your firm*. This covers those benefits that are not actually exclusive to your firm, and then look for those that are, and do not exclude the obvious like town centre parking, home visits or foreign language speakers.
- *Going to this particular office*. If you have more than one office let staff at each office concentrate on their own premises. Do not forget premises offer many benefits, e.g. disabled access, late night 'shopping', Saturday clinics, that are perhaps not offered firm-wide but at that office.
- *Dealing with a specific department*. Once staff have considered going to a solicitor, the firm and their office, let them concentrate on the benefits of their own individual department and its services in general.
- *Buying a specific service*. Let staff consider the benefits of the individual service or 'product' they assist to produce.
- *Relating to a specific fee earner*. Finally, let each fee earner, including partners, list the benefits that he or she personally offers to individual clients.
- *Other*. This 'catch all' heading is worth including for those obscure or 'off the wall' benefits that are often missed and sometimes add real value. Perhaps the firm or an office includes a coffee machine in reception, or has text message alerts when key stages in the client's transaction are reached. There will be many 'little' benefits that the firm offers and truly the little things matter.

Essentially you are looking to 'brainstorm' all the benefits of going to your firm. These do not have to be exclusive to your firm. Even though all practices will undoubtedly speak of 'qualified and experienced staff', there is no reason for you to leave it out as it is a genuine benefit you have to offer too.

The analysis and collation of the returned forms (see **Annex 1B**) will reduce the likely repetition and enable the collator and partners to extend the benefits into a format that will be meaningful to potential clients and recommenders. Then the staff should be told the results and thanked for their participation.

It is important how the benefits are presented. Each benefit needs the 'So what?' test applied. 'You will deal with our qualified and experienced conveyancing staff' could lead to 'So what?'. 'You will not have an untrained junior dealing with your matter', might be the answer. But, the real benefit to the client is likely to be expressed by a phrase such as 'This means to you that ...'. Perhaps, 'This means to you that our experienced team are in contact with all other parties involved in the transaction on a regular basis, have conveyed property like this, in this area for 20 years and know what to look out for'.

In a personal conversation one might go on to ask a question to cement the relationship and ensure the client understanding, such as 'That's better than having it transacted by an unknown person over the internet/in another town/by a supermarket isn't it?'

The various methods for the presentation of benefits are covered in many of the following chapters, but the first stage is the benefit analysis, which needs to be looked at in comparison with the 'new competition', those large non-solicitor providers of legal services. Earlier we discussed the negative start point of the profession; this negative also applies to that competition. Legal services are a derived, rarely required 'product'. The 'new competition' strive to overcome this with repetitive regular promotion of their benefits. They spend millions of pounds doing this on a national basis, but you can do the same on a very reasonable budget by sticking to your own geographical market or target segment and presenting relevant benefits in a regular but targeted way.

This will be covered in **Chapter 14,** but it is important to undertake benefits analysis as a first step to identify the advantages you have over these new, big competitors. (Hopefully, the following advantages will appear as benefits on a least some of your staff benefit analysis return forms.)

You have a genuine, general public demand. Every survey supports the continuation of an independent legal profession. Of course, there are reservations. The profession is often unfairly judged as expensive, a wrong opinion seized upon by the 'new competition' and exploited. In some cases, solicitors are considered non-communicative to the point of being stand-offish. This is all easily overcome with a proactive approach.

In truth, the 'new competition' are an (as yet) unknown quantity, formed from good brand images but in unrelated fields. By contrast, the profession is known to be heavily supervised and regulated by the Solicitors Regulation Authority (SRA). It is made up of qualified people who are specialists and have extensive experience in their fields.

Another benefit is that many firms can boast of experience in their town or area going back decades or more. When expressed as a 'this means to you...' benefit, it is very reassuring and powerful (e.g. local knowledge, local experience, etc.). This local presence is an extremely important benefit to someone local selecting a supplier, but the prospect must be told and have the benefits to them explained and enlarged upon.

It is not just long standing local knowledge and contacts, important though these are; it is also what might be described as 'pop-in ability'. The huge value of the local firm, especially those who rise to the challenge and offer 24/7 contact through the internet, is this additional local presence and the ability it provides to call in by appointment, or even on the off chance. No big, centrally based provider can offer this.

Local presence extends beyond the obvious professional contacts. A firm is likely to be well known locally and will be seen as part of the community, something that it shares with its potential and actual clients. A local firm knows the area and is known in the area; it understands its positives and its negatives and everyone likes to go where they are understood, and where they feel at home.

Annex 1A
Benefit analysis return form

Further to the attached memo [*see Annex 1C*] relating to our benefits analysis, could you please complete and return this form to me within the next two weeks.

If you have any queries please do not hesitate to contact your departmental head, or me directly.

As noted in the attached memo, we consider this analysis to be extremely important for the development of the firm and your participation is fully appreciated.

As you will see, the analysis is broken down into seven headings which we would like you to consider as fully and as widely as possible. There cannot be too many answers and there are no wrong answers. Nobody is being judged by this exercise which we hope will ultimately be of value to us all.

Question 6 relates to fee earners and needs to be completed by them only.

---

1. What are the benefits to a client of going to a solicitor?

[*When answering this question, remember that these days there are many alternatives open to potential clients. However, the legal profession has many benefits to offer over and above this 'new competition'. What, in your opinion are these benefits?*]

---

2. What are the benefits of going to your firm?

[*Please be wide ranging in your thoughts on this. It really will be very helpful. Please include any benefits that you may feel are general to all legal practices and not specific to ours. They are all nonetheless benefits that we have to offer.*]

---

3. What are the benefits of going to your individual office?

[*Only applicable if your firm has two or more premises. Please concentrate on your office. What benefits does it have to offer over and above those already offered by the firm in general?*]

---

4. What are the benefits of dealing with a specific department?

[*Having looked at the benefits appertaining to solicitors, this firm and individual offices, please consider the department in which you work. What benefits does your department offer over and above those already listed?*]

---

5. What are the benefits of buying a specific service?

[*Please consider the benefits of the individual service or 'product' that you assist to produce.*]

6. What are the benefits relating to a specific fee earner?

[*This section is intended to be completed by fee earners only and relates to the benefits offered by their specific activity and approach and by them/you personally.*]

7. Others benefits:

[*Can you think of any benefits that are not listed above? If so, please include them here. It is sometimes these 'obscure' benefits that are the greatest value of all.*]

Thank you for your assistance in this important task and I confirm that when the results have been analysed you will be informed of them.

May I emphasise again that there is no judgment whatsoever being applied to your answers. There are no wrong answers and your assistance is valued.

Annex 1B
Benefits analysis consolidation form

Benefit	What this benefit means to the client
1. The benefits of going to a solicitor (any solicitor):	
2. The benefits of going to your individual firm:	
3. The benefits of visiting a specific office (assuming you have more than one office):	
4. The benefits of dealing with a specific department:	
5. The benefits of buying a specific service from your firm:	
6. The benefits related to specific individual fee earners:	
7. Other benefits:	

Annex 1C
Letter/email to all staff re: benefit analysis template

To: All members of staff

From: [*Senior/marketing partner*]

Subject: What is it we provide to our clients?

As part of our continuing work on practice development and marketing, we are looking at the benefits to our clients of the firm's work and activity for them. To understand this better we need to ask each member of staff to think about what it is that we provide for our clients by way of benefits derived from our services. The aim is to produce a list of benefits to be used across the firm and in future promotional activity. Attached is a questionnaire that outlines what it is we are looking for and the areas we would like you to consider. Once completed we will be collating the questionnaires so please do write as many benefits as occur to you. There are no wrong answers. Since everyone will be completing this form we understand that there will be repetition from people in the same department. This is quite acceptable and will be sorted out during collation. We would expect you to spend half an hour or less. If you get 'writer's block', please call me for inspiration.

To help identify benefits, below is a list of reasons why people or companies use solicitors. Think how and where these apply to our firm.

* Help in solving problems (getting out of trouble).
* Help in preventing problems.
* Money – ways to save it, keep it or make it.
* Background – experience or expertise in a particular matter.
* Background – experience or expertise in a client's industry or field (in the case of commercial clients).
* Attention and respect to the client.
* Availability to the client.
* New ideas for the client.
* Timeliness.
* Confidence that provides the client with peace of mind.
* A big name in the area or a recognised expert in their field (e.g. we are).
* Being kept informed throughout.
* Detailed follow-up.
* General business counsel (in the case of commercial clients).
* General personal counsel (in the case of private clients – as it was in the days of the 'family solicitor' or the 'man of affairs').
* Value. This does not mean cheapest – it means understanding the benefits being paid for.
* The right chemistry. Everyone in every organisation has a profile. The trick is to fit ours to theirs.

2 Tools to help you prepare to market your practice

One of the common myths about marketing is that the words 'marketing' and 'promotion' are interchangeable: that they are in effect the same thing with two different name tags. This is not only incorrect but also, potentially, quite dangerous. Historically, too many legal practices feel they have 'done their marketing' when they have bought some advertising space and put up a website, but they have actually done no marketing at all, just a little promotion.

This chapter looks at the tasks that any marketing manager would undertake and relates them to the legal profession. Many readers will be familiar with, or at least aware of, the exercises we propose you undertake for your firm, but experience suggests that few solicitors complete them as fully as is recommended. Hopefully, the following will help you to do so and, with reference to our opening remarks, you will note that promotion comes last in what might be termed the 'marketing chain'. There is much for the marketing partner to do before spending the promotional budget.

Before proceeding, it is perhaps appropriate to consider the role of the 'marketing partner'. Most commercial enterprises have, in one form or another, what we would term a 'board of directors'. It is, of course, mandatory for a limited company to have directors, but all commercial entities have to perform the roles found in a board of directors. Here there will usually be a production director, an accounts and financial director, a marketing director and a managing director or chairperson who coordinates everything and oversees strategy.

A legal firm is no different. To production may be added recruitment, training and compliance; financial has the added legal cashier requirements and responsibilities; and the 'managing director' will almost certainly continue to be a fee earner. The 'marketing director/partner' has the responsibilities, if our definition in the Preface is accepted, for everything in the firm that does not involve production or accounts.

There are two points to consider. First, not all the above roles have to be undertaken by partners. Increasingly, we see associate solicitors in executive roles. Second, some firms are too small to provide so many executives. It is advisable, however, that the management of all practices look at their firms from the three discreet viewpoints of production, accounts and marketing, and deal with them as separate issues. A further consideration is that the marketing discipline is even more vital to the smaller firm or sole practitioner, as it may be the route to not only growth but initially, in some cases, to survival.

There are three areas of analysis that the marketing partner should undertake:

- A SWOT (strengths, weaknesses, opportunities and threats) analysis.
- A PESTLE (political, economic, social, technological, legal, environmental) analysis.
- A six 'Ps' (product, place, price, profit, people, promotion) analysis.

2.1 The SWOT analysis

The marketing partner may consider involving the staff in the SWOT analysis as was done with the firm's benefit analysis in **Chapter 1**. We would advise against this, as it will seem repetitive to staff and in any case the results of the benefit analysis will lead clearly to strengths and opportunities, if not weaknesses and threats.

The SWOT analysis should be undertaken at a partners' or executive meeting and be led and minuted by the marketing partner.

Because your firm is inextricably linked to the profession, your own SWOT analysis will be incomplete without a SWOT analysis of the profession overlaid on it.

In both cases, strengths and weaknesses are internal factors, with opportunities and threats external.

As a rule it is always best to expend resource (time, money, people) on bolstering strengths and following up opportunities, while being aware of weaknesses (addressing or accommodating them) and watchful of threats (reacting as needed).

Below you will find an example of both SWOTs. Be aware that these are only indicative. Both are far from complete and neither can represent your firm or your thinking. Your firm's SWOT, to have any value, must be done by you. The template in **Annex 2A** can be used for this purpose.

2.1.1 SWOT analysis of the legal profession in England and Wales

Your practice is inextricably part of the highly institutionalised legal profession which is governed, in England and Wales, by the Solicitors Regulation Authority (SRA) and is under the influence of the Law Society and the government. Actions taken by an individual firm will always be in the larger overall context of the profession itself, and it is therefore essential to look first at the SWOTs of the profession.

You should undertake your own analysis of the profession using the template, but this indicative analysis is hopefully a start point.

Internal factors

Strengths:

- Independence.
- Known integrity.
- Known strict code of conduct.
- Respected.
- Some 'monopolies' (e.g. crime).
- Obligatory negligence insurance.
- Strong public demand for the continuance of an independent legal profession.

Weaknesses:

- Restrictions of that code of conduct.
- Historic dependence upon 'bread and butter' products (conveyancing, probate, etc.).
- Perceived inapproachability.
- Perceived high level of fees.
- Relative lack of commercial skills.
- Non-specialist tradition.
- History of regulated (monopolistic) markets.
- Fragmented structure.
- Slow to change.
- Ignorance of the 'new competition'.
- Uncertainty/lack of response to the 'new competition'.
- Focus on matters and not on clients.

External factors

Opportunities:

- Established and growing potential market for legal services.
- Complexity of the legal environment.
- Europe/increasing globalisation.
- Scope for innovation.
- Association with or forming of multi-disciplinary practices.
- Legal Services Act 2007 (including alternative business structures (ABSs)).
- Consumers and small businesses ignorance of the value of solicitors' work.
- The internet and social media.

Threats:

- New commercially-aware competitors.
- Aggressive promotional stance of competitors (deliberately challenging the traditional legal practice).
- Loss of 'bread and butter' matters leading to a considerable reduction in fee revenue.
- Loss of referral fees.

- Legal aid franchises and rates.
- Small Claims Court.
- Ongoing reviews forcing change (such as the Clementi and Carter reviews).
- Continuing government spending pressure on publicly funded work.
- Legal Services Act 2007.
- The internet.

2.1.2   A SWOT analysis of your firm (example)

The following is an example only. Clearly, what is important here is your own analysis of your firm.

Internal factors

Strengths:

- Highly motivated staff.
- Wide range of services provided to private clients.
- Limited but focused range of services provided to commercial clients.
- High levels of technical competence among fee earners.
- Financial reserves.
- Reputation.
- Location of offices.
- Strong network of referrers.

Weaknesses:

- Lack of coordinated marketing plan.
- Insufficient investment in marketing and promotional activities.
- Poor cash flow.
- Lack of control over disbursements.
- Ineffective use of key performance indicators.

External factors

Opportunities:

- Alternative business structures.
- Ageing population.
- Wills and probate work.
- Acquisition or merger.
- Outcomes-focused regulation.
- Targeted promotional activity.
- Greater development of the 'professional contacts register' (see **Chapter 6**).

Threats:

- Alternative business structures.
- Flat/declining housing market.
- The 'new competition'.
- E-law.
- Bank lending restrictions.
- Public sector funding cuts.
- Increasingly restrictive lenders panels.
- Erosion of potential market by the aggressive commercially aware 'new competition'.

2.2 PESTLE analysis

The purpose of a PESTLE analysis is to review the outside factors that may have an influence on your firm. Generally speaking these are factors that are on a 'grander' scale than those found in a SWOT analysis. The degree to which your firm is affected by PESTLE findings will depend partly on its size, location and areas of activity. Without exception, however, it is worth all firms undertaking this analysis as part of their marketing activity and certainly in advance of any promotional activity.

A PESTLE analysis may well indicate where the firm should be going with its existing resources or resources that can be acquired. The world is a constantly changing place and a PESTLE analysis can help you keep up with these changes.

2.2.1 PESTLE analysis – examples of influencing factors

As with the SWOT analysis example above, this is by no means an exhaustive list and clearly will not apply specifically to your firm.

Political

- Stability of government.
- Position of UK in Europe.
- Attitude to public and private sectors.
- Attitude to external regulation.
- Attitude to the professional sector.
- Influence of UK regions and regional grants.
- Increase in global interaction.

Economic

- Current economic performance and predictions.
- Long-term economy.

- Business performance.
- Government policies.
- Fiscal policies.
- Interest rates.
- EU influence.
- Global influence.
- IT impact.
- Current public perception of services.
- Skills shortages.

Social

- Gap between rich and poor.
- Shift in work patterns.
- More working women.
- Familiarity with IT.
- Increase in direct purchases.
- Increase in consumerism.
- Increase in location independence.
- Decline in job security.
- Increase in number of self-employed.
- Increase in leisure time.
- Increase in divorce/single parents.
- Decline in school leavers and standards.
- Increase in higher education.
- Social diversity.
- Ageing population.

Technological

- Increase in speed of change.
- Increase in dependence on technology.
- Worldwide access via internet.
- Speed of access/business response.
- Improved/cheaper communication.
- Reduced costs.
- Impact on way of working/skills shift.
- Skills shortage.
- 24-hour access.
- Impact on accessing products/services.

Legal

- Volume of legislation.
- Complexity of legislation.
- Increase in layers of influence – regional, national, Europe, global.
- Increase in consumerism.

- Increase in public access to information.
- Increase in sophistication of clients.
- Decrease in any client loyalty to a specific firm.

Environmental

- Increasing emphasis in business context.
- Increasing legislation.
- Decline in quality of environment.
- Pressure on finite resources.
- Potential climate change.
- Increase in importance of water.
- Increase in demands for energy.

The template in **Annex 2B** can be used to form the basis of your own PESTLE analysis.

2.3 The six 'Ps' (product, place, price, profit, people, promotion) analysis

The final analysis proposed for the marketing partner to undertake is a classic way of analysing any commercial entity but is particularly appropriate to the legal profession.

The example given in **Annex 2C** can be used to assist in this analysis in conjunction with the explanatory text below.

2.3.1 Product

It may seem obvious but the first thing to list is the full range of products offered by the firm. It is proposed that the firm's services are broken down into as many 'products' as possible, so that conveyancing would become, at the least, sales; purchase; sale and purchase; investment purchase; buy to let purchase; investment sale; buy to let sale; remortgage; and repossession.

The next stage is to describe each 'product' in terms of what it provides for the client.

The profession is inclined to think procedurally. Clients do not buy procedures any more than they buy solicitors' time. They purchase the benefits and need to understand them. Therefore, the next stage is to ensure that every product has a list of benefits next to it. It is these benefits that will form the basis of promotion. (See also **Chapter 1**.)

If the firm has individual departments, it is best to involve the departmental heads in this analysis.

Analysis needs to also include the standard of service that is being offered (expensive and exclusive, or cheap and high volume, etc.); the options that may be offered, for example, a fixed fee base product to which optional extras are added; the capacity the firm has currently or could acquire to deliver this product, in other words what is the maximum that can be achieved in production terms, and within consideration of product there is a need to think in terms of branding, presentation; and how complaints would be handled.

Although it seems unlikely in terms of legal products, the product life cycle is worth considering and one only has to look at the decline in various matter types to see why. Essentially, there are four stages in a product life cycle: the introduction of the product, the growth and development of that product, the maturity of the product and finally its decline. It is necessary to consider where on that life cycle each product is.

There are many practices that offer legal services, including the 'new competition'. Consideration needs to be given to product differentiation so that you are not offering a 'me too' product. Look at your benefit analysis: what is special about what you have to offer?

Apart from differentiating your product range from others, there is also the opportunity of 'extending' a product by the addition of extra services or features, or by linking services together for a specific market (e.g. conveyancing and wills, or wills and EPAs). Home visits and out of hours appointments would extend the benefits being offered by a particular product, and indeed probably differentiate your service from those offered by others.

Finally under product, in terms of the firm-wide development ambitions, what are your 'prime products'? Which are the products that you will concentrate on? These should be products that are demonstrably profitable, for which you have existing capacity to expand or are able to acquire that capacity, which have a proven need in the marketplace and for which you have direct access to that market. These should be products that are demonstrably in demand and, with help from your promotional activity, understood by the potential client.

2.3.2 Place

Historically, from a marketing point of view, 'place' would have meant an assessment of how the office looks and how clients are treated at the beginning of their 'client journey'. This is of course still valid today. However, under the 'place' heading you must now also consider how you appear on your website, which is, of course, a portal to your firm, and the presence you have on social networking sites and the firm's policy regarding this new and free media. You also need to consider where else you are going to make yourself available to potential clients, be it via seminars, webinars, exhibitions, clinics or of course your promotional material.

2.3.3 Price

Historically within the profession, pricing has always tended towards a cost plus basis. Today it is also important to consider market influences as consumer awareness, competition and other factors may force a reduction in price. However, differentiation, presentation of quality benefits and offering extra value may provide opportunity for price increase. It should not be forgotten that price makes a strong statement about quality. High price, providing it is sustainable, can reduce the need for volume whereas price cutting can only be achieved if volume is markedly increased. The marketing manager needs to consider this pricing strategy while recognising that the pricing adopted by one department can have an influence over the impression given by the others.

Another pricing consideration must be fixed fees. For some time now the presentation of an hourly rate has caused suspicion. Clearly there are some disciplines where this must be maintained and others where it can still be achieved, but a fixed fee offer, most likely along with optional extras, is a pricing approach that is more clearly understood by the public and viewed with far less suspicion. It should be noted that it is also the approach being adopted by a large section of the 'new competition'.

2.3.4 Profit

There are still many firms today who understand the overall profitability of their practice without fully appreciating where that profit comes from or where profit is being lost. An early task for the marketing manager must be a profit analysis of the firm, but also of individual departments, individual 'products' within that department and possibly even individual fee earners. Only when a firm is completely clear where profit is coming from, can it clearly define the prime products and the key promotional areas. The main hurdle in undertaking a profitability study would seem to be the creation of a formula for apportioning overheads. The simplest method would be to ignore fixed overheads (unless they can be demonstrably cut back by the reduction of a particular department) and to undertake an analysis of the actual overheads, allowing for the inclusion of a contribution to fixed overheads and fees to the department or fee earner and the management costs.

2.3.5 People

If there is one enterprise that can truly be said to be based upon 'people', it is the legal profession.

Chapter 3 looks at staff as a marketing resource, but at this stage it is worth considering the following questions:

- What do your staff say to clients?
- What do your staff say socially about the firm?
- Do your staff share the partnership vision?

- Do your staff understand their role and place in this vision?
- How are your staff rewarded (this is not just a question of money)?
- Are your staff the first or the last to know about new promotional campaigns?
- Do staff meetings allow for a two-way flow of ideas?
- Does the firm remember to say 'thank you' to staff?

2.3.6 Promotion

As has been noted previously, there is a great deal of work to be undertaken before we get to 'promotion'.

That said, at this stage, the marketing partner should undertake an analysis of what promotion the firm currently does, pass an opinion on its effectiveness, value for money and overall appearance and perhaps seek fresh ideas from certain members of staff.

Promotional activity and ideas are discussed in more detail at **Chapters 7** and **14.**

Annex 2A
SWOT analysis form

SWOT analysis of the legal profession in England and Wales

Internal factors	
Strengths	Weaknesses

External factors	
Opportunities	Threats

SWOT analysis of your firm

Internal factors	
Strengths	Weaknesses

External factors	
Opportunities	Threats

Annex 2B
PESTLE analysis form

PESTLE analysis – influencing factors

Political

Economic

Social

Technological

Legal

Environmental

Annex 2C
The six 'Ps' analysis

Product

- What is the range (of services) offered by the firm?
- What are the 'sub-products'? (The services of the firm broken down further to individual 'products'.)
- What are the benefits (of each service)?
- What is the standard/level of service offered by the firm?
- Where is each product in its product life cycle?
- How can products be differentiated?
- How can products be extended?
- What are the firm's prime products?

Place

- How does the office really look inside and out?
- How does the firm's website compare with local competition (new and traditional)?
- Can/does the firm hold client seminars/webinars?
- Can/does the firm offer clinics or late night/weekend opening?
- What exhibitions should the firm attend?
- How does the firm's literature compare with others?

Price

- What is the firm's pricing strategy?
- When did the firm last undertake a price comparison (with the competition)?
- Which of the firm's products could (possibly) be suitable for a fixed fee approach?

Profit

- When was a true profit analysis last undertaken?
- When will this be updated with reference to the profitability of:
    - the firm?
    - each office?
    - each department?
    - each fee earner?

People

Consider the following:

- What do staff say to clients?
- What do staff say socially about the firm?
- Do the staff share the partnership vision?
- Do they understand their role and place in this vision?
- How are they rewarded (this is not just a question of money)?
- Are they the first or the last to know about new promotional campaigns?
- Do staff meetings allow for a two-way flow of ideas?
- Does the firm remember to say 'thank you' to the staff?

Promotion

- What current promotional activity does the firm undertake?
- What are the costs of this activity?
- What are the results of this activity and how are they measured?
- How does the firm's promotional activity compare with the competition (both new and traditional)?
- What promotional activity should the firm be undertaking?

3 Your staff as a marketing resource

Chapter 1 discussed involving staff in the firm's benefit analysis and **Chapter 2** covered the importance of your people, your staff, as part of the six 'Ps'. This chapter looks at the potential for this important part of your firm to be a marketing resource.

This is not to say that everyone should become a sales person. Some would not be able to, many would not want to, and any number would justifiably say 'it is not my job'. What we are proposing is that you should assist your staff to present the benefits that they have helped to define, while ensuring they are clear about the firm's objectives and plans and understand exactly where they fit into them. It is important to seek their support in the firm's endeavours and when most people feel 'needed' they respond well.

Firms need to emphasise how important the client is and how everybody within the firm can affect how a client views the firm. Firms need to help everyone to understand 'opportunity recognition' and what to do when an opportunity is recognised. Most people understand 'cross-selling' and this is the start point of it. 'Price justification' is another important area. How do your staff react when a friend states 'solicitors are jolly expensive'? Can they handle this question or do they simply say 'Yes, and the pay is lousy too!'

Important information and many good ideas are lost simply because the partners and management of firms do not talk to their staff, ask the right questions or perhaps listen. Firms need to produce a conduit for ideas and information, a sort of high tech 'suggestion box'.

3.1 Involving your staff

Our strongest recommendation here is that once your strategic, marketing and promotional plans are clear, your staff should be fully informed of them and their place within the plans. What you are seeking is your staff's commitment to the success of these plans.

The questionnaires in **Annex 3B** and **3C** are useful resources to aid this. **Annex 3B** contains a skills and interests audit which will help you understand your staff and their out of work activities better (and may even lead to ideas for promotional niches) and **Annex 3C** is a feedback form which will allow staff to tell you what they think of the firm and your management style.

3.2 Client care training

As is undoubtedly understood, clients are the most important asset of any practice. The security of this asset depends not only upon the quality of legal work presented, but also on how clients feel about the firm. This 'feeling' can be influenced by all and any member of staff. Therefore, training staff in client care, the way clients are looked after, cared for and dealt with, is extremely important. The Law Society publishes a number of books on this subject and there are several consultancy organisations offering outside or in-house training on this subject.

It sometimes goes unrecognised just how much damage to a firm's reputation can be the result of lack of thought or carelessness. Successful interaction with people requires a set of minimum standards. All partners, fee earners and staff in any firm have contact with, or deal with clients, even if this is incidental to their main job. All personnel therefore need to be aware of the importance of handling clients in a friendly but professional manner. Sometimes factors make that difficult and the different needs people have influence their behaviour.

It may help to impress upon all members of staff that getting the basics of client and interpersonal contact right helps the firm in several different areas:

1. Clients' impressions of the firm will be partly formed by their impression of individual staff members.
2. The reputation of the firm and therefore its future viability, is largely dependent on what clients think of your staff as individuals.
3. Your staff members' job satisfaction will be greater if they are more successful in handling clients.
4. Your staff members' jobs will in many ways be easier if they can overcome the problems sometimes associated with handling clients.
5. The firm's relationship with clients will improve, your staff members' relationship with clients will improve and this will lead to a better working environment (better understanding of each other's jobs and all pulling together for the common cause).

It is more than basic manners that are needed, it is a professional approach.

3.3 Opportunity recognition

While part of any firm's development programme will be the seeking of new clients and contacts, it is equally important to seek repeat business from existing clients. One of the biggest barriers to this is the apparent reluctance of staff to speak more fully about the many services that a firm has to offer over and beyond those with which they are actually dealing.

While it is crucial that staff members have a full understanding of all the services available from the firm and the ability to present the benefits of their services to the client, the key is recognising when there is an appropriate opportunity to present these benefits.

All fee earning and support staff must begin to think about 'cross-selling' and be fully au fait with the services offered by their firm, understand the benefits offered, know *how* to present them but above all know *when* to present them. This is opportunity recognition.

- Surely that person making a will also needs a lasting power of attorney (LPA)?
- How can you allow two people purchasing a house together to enter into this transaction without a trust deed?
- If an elderly person is selling a house, what other advice, assistance and support are required for his or her undoubted rearrangement of financial affairs?
- Is the business executive buying a house, that is going to stretch his or her resources, going to need further advice and additional services from you?
- Does a private client have the opportunity to influence the placing of commercial work, i.e. if the client is a company director, sole practitioner, self-employed, etc.?
- Is the managing director of a firm buying a factory building expanding the business and in need of employment law advice?
- Is the firm being negligent? If a client leaves the premises with a probate cheque, should the firm not be offering financial and investment advice?

There are of course many other examples.

Staff need to be encouraged to consider all the products of the firm and the opportunities that they may present. Fee earners should be asked to think about their individual disciplines and their clients and consider what other services a client may require. At the same time they should consider what work could be passed to them by other departments in the firm. An easy example would be that a conveyancer promotes will making to new house purchasers and could also be doing the conveyancing of a deceased person's house passed to them by the probate department.

3.4 Price justification

Price justification is as much about avoiding the need to justify price as it is about explanation. Whenever it occurs, and it can be a matter of timing, it is about clarity, openness, presentation and understanding.

If a fee is being challenged at the presentation of the bill and assuming the client is not one who challenges every invoice as a matter of principle, it is most probably an expression of surprise and disappointment. It should be a matter of policy to avoid a client experiencing these negative emotions.

While cost justification is not a strategic reason to adopt fixed fees, it is evident that an accepted fixed fee requires less cost justification later. A clear quotation and explanation of the variants can have the same effect.

Above all, justifying cost at the beginning of the transaction is the most likely way of ensuring client satisfaction and swift bill payment. The justification of cost stems, once again, from a clear statement of the benefits the client will receive by appointing you to do the work, along with the cost dangers of not having that work done properly. Make sure that clients are aware of the benefits and ensure they see that these benefits outweigh the charges being faced. Then you have achieved cost justification at the right time – at the beginning of the job.

Remember, legal work is a derived need and most people have no idea what they are paying for in real terms. It is the firm's job is to tell them and in a way that they understand.

3.5   A conduit for ideas and information

In this chapter we have been talking about your staff as a marketing resource. With encouragement and a clear conduit of information, they can be a source of information and ideas, a support to the overall objectives of the firm and representatives of the firm to the outside world. Too many firms still have the 'them and us' syndrome, which has no place in an environment where staff are trying to all work together.

Consider this: is your firm ruled by memo or conversation? Is it run through emails or meetings?

As part of the overall analysis the marketing partner is undertaking, consideration should be given to the list of questions in **Annex 3D.**

As can probably be deduced from that list, we would recommend regular, possibly quarterly, full staff meetings, based entirely upon informing the staff of the firm's progress, introducing new initiatives and allowing an opportunity for information to be provided by the staff. Of course, emails still have an important role in today's world and are the best method of distributing memos, especially if they are the minutes of a meeting.

Sometimes staff are reticent and the old fashioned idea of a 'suggestion box' is not such a bad one. Today it is probably likely to be emails sent to a dedicated internal email address such as 'ideas@[*name of firm*].co.uk'.

Annex 3A

Skills and interests form – informative note to staff

The partners are currently involved in planning the firm's strategic development and growth over the next few years in light of the recent changes we have experienced within the profession.

It is a policy decision to involve all staff in this planning process and you will in due course be asked to complete a questionnaire that will be discussed with you individually. The value of this exercise should not be underestimated. The results, once analysed, will be published along with the strategic decisions that have been made as a result of the findings.

It is very important that no one should view this exercise with doubt or suspicion. It is, and is intended to be, both positive and forward looking as well as a prelude to a period of growth. You will be kept informed at each stage and it is part of our stated objective to improve the security, working conditions and future of all employees. If you have any queries relating to this letter, or the form that will be distributed within a week or two, please do not hesitate to ask me personally.

Annex 3B
Skills and interests audit form

Dear [*name*]

Further to the memo referring to the firm's strategic planning programme, I have pleasure in attaching the skills and interests audit form.

There are no right or wrong answers. Please only take 10 to 15 minutes to fill in the form – brief answers are perfectly acceptable. Please then return the form to me.

Note this is a voluntary exercise. Your help would be greatly appreciated, however, do feel free to leave blanks on the form if you feel that the question is inappropriate.

Name	
Job title	
Department	
Specialist area of law (if a fee earner)	
Specialist area of work (if support staff)	
Home address and post code	
Spouse's name	
Spouse's occupation	
Children(s) name(s) and age(s)	

Other work or previous employment experience (whether in the legal profession or not)
Other work or professional activities (e.g. boards, committees, directorships, trusts or council activities)
Trade association memberships, club memberships (e.g. theatrical, chess, reading circles) or sports club memberships
Charitable/community/civic activities
Spouse's memberships and activities
Other interests and hobbies

Spouse's interests and hobbies
Favourite client by name and by type
Key prospects
Personal strengths
Ambitions

Please note that information provided on this form is held on an informal basis and will form no part of your employment record or be used in any way as an appraisal.

Annex 3C
Staff feedback questionnaire form

The recent activity, in which we have all been involved, is geared to improve the firm's performance and to ready it for a period of growth, leading to a more secure future for all of us.

Now it is the turn of the firm's management to be put under scrutiny. We are most interested in your views and we are sure that you will be open and honest. To assist this you may, without any concern, return the form anonymously.

1. What are the best things in your opinion about this firm?

2. What would you say the 'values' of the firm are?

3. What is not so good about the firm and why?

4. If there were three things about the firm you could change, what would they be?

1.

2.

3.

5. How well do you think the firm is managed?

6. Which of the following, in your opinion, apply to the firm.

	Strongly agree	Agree	Disagree	Strongly disagree	Don't know
The practice has a positive culture	☐	☐	☐	☐	☐
The senior management team work well together	☐	☐	☐	☐	☐
There is a clear business plan for the practice's development	☐	☐	☐	☐	☐
I understand the practice's business plan and my part in it	☐	☐	☐	☐	☐
Communications between management and staff are good	☐	☐	☐	☐	☐
Communications between departments are good	☐	☐	☐	☐	☐
Communications between offices (if appropriate) are good	☐	☐	☐	☐	☐

The senior management team are highly motivated	☐	☐	☐	☐	☐
Fee earners are highly motivated	☐	☐	☐	☐	☐
Support staff are highly motivated	☐	☐	☐	☐	☐
The practice is well managed	☐	☐	☐	☐	☐
My skills are utilised to the full	☐	☐	☐	☐	☐
The practice is good at training and developing staff	☐	☐	☐	☐	☐
The practice's appraisal system works well	☐	☐	☐	☐	☐
The practice is good at marketing	☐	☐	☐	☐	☐
The practice is good at cross-selling	☐	☐	☐	☐	☐
The practice delivers high quality client care	☐	☐	☐	☐	☐
The practice is good at responding to enquiries from prospective clients	☐	☐	☐	☐	☐
The practice has a good reputation	☐	☐	☐	☐	☐
The practice makes good use of IT	☐	☐	☐	☐	☐
The practice's file management procedures are good	☐	☐	☐	☐	☐

7. What is the practice's current reputation? How do you think clients or professional contacts would describe the firm?

8. What is your vision of the firm in five years' time? What should we be aiming for in terms of markets, reputation and profile?

9. Are there any practices which you consider are good role models for this firm to emulate?

Annex 3D
Staff communications analysis checklist

- How regularly are staff meetings held?
- What form do these meetings take?
- Are they departmental or firm-wide?
- Are the staff managed by memo/email or through face-to-face meetings?
- Does the firm have an appraisal system?
- What form does this appraisal system take?
- How often are appraisals held?
- What is the conduit for ideas to be passed up to management from the staff?
- What is the conduit for information to be passed down from management to the staff?
- How are new promotional initiatives, such as the publication of a newsletter, introduced to staff?
- How involved are members of the staff in the creation of these initiatives?
- How au fait are the staff with the principles of marketing and the firm's growth plans?
- Which of the staff show particular promise and interest in this area?
- When and how will the partnership declare the results of the skills and interests audit to the staff?
- When and how will the partners declare the results of the other information that has been requested from and provided by the staff?

4 Selling more to existing clients

This chapter and **Chapter 5** essentially look at 'growing your firm'. It is assumed that the need for growth is understood. If you stand still you will effectively enter a downward spiral as the environment in which you operate changes, your competition grows, adapts and develops, the market for your services expands without you and the competition for high quality staff increases.

Growth and expansion is often seen as impossibly expensive. This is not so. A simple approach to expansion could be, and often is, described in marketing jargon as 'vertical and horizontal expansion'.

In its simplest form, vertical expansion is the selling of new or additional products to existing clients, while horizontal expansion is the *active* seeking of recommendations and other routes to new clients. The majority of legal firms would claim that a substantial amount of their new business comes from recommendations, but few *actively* seek them. This is discussed in more detail in **Chapter 5** and indeed in **Chapter 6,** however the basic principles of this are listed below.

To expand vertically and horizontally demands a starting point and that is your client database. Your past, satisfied clients are the seedcorn to your future.

If you do not have a client database, or at the minimum an accurate and up-to-date mailing list, stop reading and create one – nothing is more important to your future. It is that important because growth and expansion need not be 'impossibly expensive' if you take the route outlined in the next three chapters – via both vertical and horizontal expansion.

Earlier in this toolkit we talked about the 'new competition'. This has now been around long enough to be simply called 'the competition' but we continue to use 'new' to differentiate it from 'traditional' competition, primarily other solicitors.

The problem with the 'new competition' is that they are regularly promoting themselves to your client base. Perhaps you have not noticed this, but because they write to their customers and clients on a very regular basis, with renewal notices, policies, holiday offers, confirmations, invoices, reminders, bookings, statements and much else, it is easy and relatively inexpensive for them to promote their legal services at the same time, often quite aggressively and sometimes to the detriment of the standing of the 'high street solicitor'. The key is regularity: they communicate regularly and are very adept at highlighting the benefits they claim to offer. In the worst case scenario the last communication a past client would have received from your firm was an invoice. It is important to do better than this and to remember that communication is the key.

It is both easier and far cheaper to keep 'old friends' than to make new ones. 'Old friends', a firm's past satisfied clients, are by far the most likely to use that firm again and recommend them, if they are encouraged to do so. Firms must plan how they will communicate with their past clients, what they will say to them and how they will encourage them to think of the firm as 'their solicitors'.

In later chapters we will look at:

- literature kits (see **Chapter 11**);
- newsletters (see **Chapter 10**);
- advertising (see **14.1**);
- sponsorship (see **14.3**);
- client registration schemes (see **Chapter 12**);
- product-specific promotion (e.g. a divorce helpline) (see **7.2**);
- market-specific promotion (e.g. for the elderly market, a 'Planning ahead for a comfortable later life' booklet) (see **7.3**);
- press and public relations (see **14.2**);
- personal 'selling' and networking (see **Chapter 15**);
- emails and e-shots (see **Chapter 10**);
- websites and social media (see **Chapter 9**).

All of these will help in the cause of vertical and horizontal expansion but all this will take time. So first return to that 'seedcorn' and your client database.

It is never too soon to start, even if all you have is a mailing list, or just the fee billing list from accounts. But you have to start somewhere.

The list contained in **Annex 4A** is intended to allow you to pull together the information necessary to personalise the standard letter presented for consideration in **Annex 4B**. It contains explanatory text and examples.

Annex 4B contains an illustrative standard letter that you could adapt for your own purposes. This letter could be sent out while you build your true database – it is never too soon to start.

Annexes 4C and **4D** contain inputting forms that you could use for private and commercial clients.

This toolkit has highlighted the need to ensure that cross-selling within a firm, between offices, perhaps, but essentially between departments, is encouraged or insisted upon, explained to fee earners and support staff and made easy within the firm. Some firms reward this activity, but this is a matter for your internal consideration.

The checklist in **Annex 4E** is intended to aid firms and simplify this task.

All these templates are intended to be illustrative not definitive. They should be used for adaptation rather than replication.

Annex 4A
Information collation list

---

1. How many entries are on your mailing list?

[Mailings of this kind are expensive. They are best undertaken, for example 1,000 at a time and the results measured. The aim is to end up with a true database of loyal/registered/reliable clients who 'automatically' use/recommend your firm.]

---

2. How close to a 'real' client database are you?

[Review the information you actually hold about your clients and compare this information with the outline inputting forms in Annexes 4C and 4D.]

---

3. What will be your 'strong opening'?

[You need to grab the attention of the readers. Why have you written to them? Why should they bother to read your standard letter? What will they gain by reading this letter?]

---

4. What are your 'prime products'?

[While promoting your full range of services, you need to concentrate on those that you most wish to sell.

For example:

Domestic conveyancing

Wills and LPAs

Totting up offences]

---

5. What are the key benefits you have to offer your clients?

[For example:

(a)   As a firm of solicitors.
- *In the area for a long time – know it well*
- *New members of the team*
- *Saturday clinics*

(b)   Your services.
- *Transaction reports*
- *Home visits for wills, etc.*
- *Avoiding the loss of your licence]*

6. What excess capacity do you have for each of your prime products?

[*What quantity of each of your products could you produce from your existing (or obtainable) resources – profitably?*]

7. What special offer/feature do you have for your past clients?

[*This may be an emphasis on a benefit range or one of the 'unique sales propositions' featured by your firm.*

For example:

- *Affairs assessment scheme*
- *A free will with conveyancing*
- *Seminars*]

8. What future promise can you make?

[*A promise is something that must be kept. Divide your future plans into definite actions that will be taken, and hopes. For the purposes of this exercise, ignore dreams.*

For example:

- *Client registration scheme*
- *Regular newsletters*
- *Appropriate seminars*]

9. What other information should/could you include in the letter?

[*This is clearly a brainstorming exercise but do not use it to produce 'padding'.*

For example:

- *New status (e.g. LLP or Limited Company)*
- *New recruits/arrivals*
- *Announcement of specialist services for the elderly client market*]

10. What is the letter's 'call to action' going to be?

[*As with benefit presentation, if the recipient says 'So what?' you have failed and your letter will probably be discarded. You must encourage the reader to do something, even if it is only 'file for future reference'. You can't win them all, but a 'call to action' will increase your chances of being remembered over time.*

You have an advantage as few people will fail to open a letter from a solicitor. But you must answer at least some of the questions above (in explanations).

'You as a valued client' is a bit old hat, but openings such as 'We have developments here that may be of interest and benefit to you' could fit the bill.

For example:

- *Become a registered client*
- *Join our affairs assessment scheme*
- *24/7 access via the internet*]

Annex 4B

Example client letter

The following letter should not be used as a standard letter. It is intended only to be an example, which you will be able to make your own, by using the information developed about your own firm in undertaking the exercise outlined in **Annex 4A**.

This letter should be personalised. One addressed to 'Dear client' will not express the interest to that client that you are trying to convey.

Dear [*name*]

[*Strong opening*]

I am pleased to be able to write to you today with some good news and I hope you will welcome this letter and find it of interest.

[*Prime products*]

As a client of [*name of firm*] you will know that we have a strong presence in the local area in the fields of conveyancing, wills, trusts and probate and family matters.

[*Key benefits (firm)*]

One of the advantages of having a solicitor is the ability to discuss matters, formally and often without charge, well before those matters become 'urgent'. We like to think that it is never too early to speak to [*name of firm*] and we welcome your visit.

[*Key benefits (services)*]

Perhaps you are considering moving home at some time in the future and want to understand more about the processes involved. We have been handling sales and purchases in this area for over 50 years now, have conveyed most types of property from cottages to mansions and know all the other professionals involved in these transactions. With this experience we will be able to provide you with the information you need.

You may think your will should be updated and even if we did not draw up your existing will, we are happy to help and advise on areas you should consider before the actual drafting begins. We are experts in the matter of trusts and inheritance tax, which you should be considering along with a lasting power of attorney, the value of which we will explain to you.

If there is one area where careful thought and advice is essential it is in family matters, especially where children are concerned. Sometimes going to a solicitor is seen as an irreversible first step to divorce. This is not the case with [*name of firm*]. At your first meeting with us, we expect to listen and advise in general terms only. Our aim will be to find the best solution for you and the most reasonable one. This meeting is always without any cost or obligation.

[*Special offer*]

To ensure that you and the other clients we have written to understand that we are trying to be proactive in our support or view, we would like to suggest you visit us for what we call an 'affairs assessment'. This meeting will be with one of our partners, or senior staff, is free of charge and will be arranged for a time that suits you. At this meeting we will discuss any matter which concerns or interests you, perhaps from the above services, or any other legal aspect of your life, including commercial work for small businesses or the self-employed.

I would want to emphasise again that there is no charge or obligation on you for undertaking an 'affairs assessment', but we believe and hope that you will find it helpful and of genuine benefit in both the long- and short-term.

[*Future promise*]

Later in the year we will be introducing a 'client registration scheme' offering advantages, additional support and benefits to our clients. It will also help us to work more closely with you and to provide a better and more targeted service. You will receive full details and those entering our 'affairs assessment' programme will get automatic registration.

[*Other information*]

It may be a relief for you to know that [*name of firm*] is a member of [*appropriate association, etc.*] and has attained the following accreditations [*list accreditations as appropriate*] as an illustration of the quality of service our clients expect.

[*Call to action*]

Thank you for reading this letter. I do hope you will join our free of charge, affairs assessment programme. To do so simply telephone [*number*], fax us on [*number*], email us at [*address*] or write a letter with your request to me personally.

My team and I look forward to being of service to you in the near future.

Yours sincerely

[*Senior managing partner*]

Annex 4C
Client database inputting form (private client)

Client number:	
Client name and title:	
Client address – including full postcode (vital for geographical sorting):	
Salutation(s):	
Occupation:	
Marital status:	
Age:	
Number of children:	
Ages of children:	
Accommodation e.g. owner occupier, freeholder, leaseholder, tenant, other:	
Mortgage – type/size:	
Will – date made, date of last codicil or update:	
Is the firm executor?	Yes ☐ No ☐
Name of other executors (have executors been contacted?):	
Introduced by:	
Partner in charge:	
Newsletter recipient:	Yes ☐ No ☐
Mailshot recipient:	Yes ☐ No ☐
Christmas card recipient:	Yes ☐ No ☐
Client matters:	
Matter number:	
Matter designation:	
Matter type code:	
Date opened:	
Date closed:	
Destroy option date:	
Estimated value:	

Actual value:	
Fee earner (code/name):	
Partner in charge (of this specific matter):	
Comments:	
Is this client in a position to influence the placing of commercial work (e.g. company director, self-employed, etc.):	

Annex 4D
Client database inputting form (commercial client)

Company name:	
Contact name 1:	
Position:	
Contact name 2:	
Position:	
Accountant:	
Year end date:	
VAT number:	
Number of employees:	
Turnover:	
SIC number:	
Business type (sole trader, limited company, plc., partnership, etc.):	
Size (number of sites):	
Shareholders or owners:	
Bank name:	
Bank branch:	
Secondary bank/branch:	
Main type of work done for client:	
Estimate of percentage of legal work instructed to other firms:	
Number of directors or employees already known to the firm (for cross referencing, the name of these contacts should be included in this inputting form):	
Email address(es) of key contacts in the company:	

Annex 4E
Cross-selling preparation checklist

- Do all appropriate staff know and understand all the services the firm offers?
- Can they recite all the benefits to the client that these services confer?
- Does each member of staff have a full range of the firm's literature and other published material, in pristine condition?
- Has this literature been fully studied?
- Is the literature fully understood?
- Has the literature and its value as a tool to cross-selling ever been discussed with them?
- Do all members of staff understand when to offer each specific 'product' (opportunity recognition)?
- Has there been any formal training in opportunity recognition?
- Do all members of staff understand the importance of the 'client journey'?
- Have staff had any formal training in client handling?
- Have staff had any formal training in benefit presentation?
- How will the firm handle a possible 'it's not my job' attitude?
- Should/does the firm offer an incentive to encourage staff to cross-sell?
- Has the firm ever held a formal meeting to introduce the subject of cross-selling to staff?
- Should such a meeting be held?
- How clear are the partners and management themselves about the importance and value of cross-selling?

5 Selling to new clients

Chapter 4 briefly discussed the need for growth and proposed the vertical and horizontal approach to it. Vertical growth (selling more services to existing clients) was reviewed in that chapter and some specific ideas were put forward. This chapter looks at horizontal expansion – *actively* seeking recommendation and other methods of securing new clients.

In truth, a lot of the activity suggested in this toolkit affects both vertical and horizontal expansion. Experience has shown that an existing client who has benefited from an 'affairs assessment' is far more likely to recommend the firm than a client of the same firm who has not been assessed. A firm's website clearly has a part to play in gaining both repeat and new business as well as newsletters, seminars, etc.

In **Chapter 6** we will suggest the establishment of a formal professional contacts register (PCR), which is a major tool in gaining recommendations and new clients, but even this will reinforce the decision of your existing clients to use you in the first place.

Perhaps the most important part of gaining and keeping new clients is the 'client journey' – how the client feels about and is treated by your firm, from seeking a solicitor in the first place, through to the completion of that first matter. Every step of this 'journey', every contact with the firm or discussion with outsiders about the firm and the client's case, every delay, every unreturned telephone call, influence how good the journey is and that will determine whether or not the firm is used again or recommended.

In fact, sadly, it will influence that decision far more than the quality of work (important though this is) because it is expected that solicitors will do a good job and there is little way of judging the standard of work anyway, but clients can judge how they are treated, which especially matters when clients are under stress.

Detailed below are the steps of the 'client journey' and what you need to consider at each stage.

5.1 Choosing your firm

5.1.1 Seeking legal help

Prospective clients will seek direction to legal firms and the 'new competition' via:

- Directories (published directories such as Yellow Pages).
- Internet advice (studying comparison listing sites, etc).

- Google and other search engines, which are by far the fastest growing way of seeking legal services.
- Advertisements. These are especially relevant with the 'new competition' and many 'below the line'.
- Direct mail. This is a common approach taken by the 'new competition' who write regularly to their existing customer bases.

(a) How well do your directory entries, internet, comparison site listings and advertisements compare with your competition, including the multi-national 'new competition'?
(b) How good is your website?

- How easy is it to navigate?
- What prominence is given to benefits over procedures?
- How easy is it to contact the firm by email and telephone from the site?

(c) What is your firm doing to actively encourage your past satisfied clients to think about your firm as 'their solicitor'?
(d) How current and impressive is your firm's literature kit (see **Chapter 11**)?

- How is it distributed to reach potential new clients?
- How is it utilised within the firm for cross-selling purposes?

5.1.2 Seeking recommendations

Prospective clients seek recommendations from:

- friends and colleagues (your old clients);
- your professional contacts register (PCR) (see **Chapter 6**);
- press articles;
- trade associations – advantageous tie-up.

(a) How are you actively encouraging your past satisfied clients to recommend you?
(b) Have you formalised the development of your own PCR?
(c) Do you have a formal and regular distribution of press articles, or a 'legal advice column'?
(d) Does your firm have any formal relationship with a 'trade association' such as a university or trade union offering an advantageous offer to their membership in the use of legal services from your firm?

5.2 First contact with the firm

This is done most often by:

- email from your website;
- email generally;
- telephone;
- calling into the office.

(a) Email is excellent but assumes a quick response. What is the system within your firm for ensuring a quick response to emails from your website and generally?

(b) How does the firm handle casual visitors, casual enquirers, those with some demonstrable concerns who arrive with or without an appointment?

5.3 Telephone contact

Generally speaking, it is evident that the first telephone contact between a client and a firm's receptionist is usually good. Unfortunately, the good impression created often gets broken down by the post-receptionist system.

You need to look at how good each department and indeed each fee earner is at taking a telephone call initially, handling it, reacting responsibly and moving the potential new client closer to the firm.

If it is appropriate, each telephone call, especially with a fee earner or senior support staff, should end in an appointment for the prospective client to visit the firm, possibly on a free of charge basis. There seems sometimes to be a reluctance to meet with anybody who cannot be billed. This is incredibly short sighted as any other organisation would see a visiting prospect as a wonderful sales opportunity. Make no mistake, the 'new competition' do.

(a) What exactly is your post-receptionist telephone system and how effective is it?

(b) How good is each department and individual fee earner at handling telephone calls from prospects? Do you have a conversion ratio to consider?

(c) Do fee earners and support staff understand the value of 'selling', or at the very least 'encouraging' appointments with prospects?

(d) What action has the firm taken to explain that unbillable appointments are of value to the firm as a form of sales activity?

5.4 First meeting

Prospects will often be nervous and ill-prepared for the first meeting. It is the responsibility of the fee earner or support staff member to ensure that the prospective client is put at ease and treated with respect.

As a generalisation, prospective clients are looking for attention and a demonstration that the fee earner has made some preparation for the meeting. They would like to come away with a feeling that they are being handled with care and respect, an explanation of the processes to be undertaken and a declaration of the problems that may be faced.

They need to be clear about what the next steps are to be, and what they and the fee earner are to do respectively, following the meeting. They need to leave this first meeting with a clear understanding of the next planned contact.

Clients, for they are clients now, must be clear about the fees to be charged and clear in their understanding of the benefits to be received that more than justify the charge being made.

(a) How good are all your fee earners (collectively and individually) at handling prospective clients during the first meeting?
(b) Can you be assured that the conclusion of the first prospect meeting will result in a clear understanding of what problems might arise, an acceptance of what the next step must be, including what the fee earner and the client has to do prior to the next meeting, and an understanding of either when that next meeting is to be or how it is to be arranged?
(c) How good are the fee earners at presenting price and cost justification?

5.5 Interim problems

It is not unusual for unforeseen problems, or new situations, to arise between the first and second meeting.

From the client's point of view how these are handled are of paramount importance.

(a) How good is your firm at handling 'interim problems'?
(b) Has the handling of 'interim problems' been discussed at all at fee earners meeting?

5.6 Second meeting

Let us assume that everything thus far has gone well. The client journey can be derailed at the second meeting if the client feels that progress has not been made, interim problems have not been handled, matters raised at the first meeting have not been addressed, queries and questions raised at the first meeting have not been answered or that anything has been left 'hanging in the air'.

On top of this there can be a tendency with fee earners to 'resent' the second meeting if they feel they are able to crack on with the case without it. It may be irrelevant to the fee earner, but it can be of major importance to the client.

(a) Has the importance of second meetings with the client ever been discussed at fee earners meetings?
(b) Are the first and second meetings minuted, and are contact reports sent to the client?

5.7 Telephone/email/letter contact and follow-ups

It is evident that in the course of handling the legal matter, communication with the client is essential. It is the communication, via whatever media, that puts clients at ease and makes them feel they are being well served and this is of paramount importance in retaining new clients and gaining subsequent work or recommendation from them.

(a) Has the firm ever considered the communications throughout a case that a fee earner has with a client from the point of view of client care and support rather than professional and procedural necessity?

(b) Surveys prove that one of the most frequent complaints about solicitors from their clients is the lack of information provided. In view of this, how good is the firm at keeping clients informed?

5.8 Promises

(a) How often does your firm make unrealistic or unnecessary promises? How clearly do you understand that a client will feel let down, even if the case is successful, if they feel (perhaps even unrealistically) that a promise has been broken?
(b) How good are you at managing client expectation and explaining, where necessary, the realities of a case?

5.9 Outcome

Clients will of course judge a firm by the successful outcome of their case or matter, but even this is a case of poor or good expectation management.

There are many cases where the firm should charge a client for telling them not to proceed. This is good legal advice, but how good is the firm at offering it?

5.10 Fees and invoices

This is expectation management yet again. It is only an unexpectedly large fee that causes argument and resentment. The emphasis here must be on 'unexpected'. Fees are not queried if they are understood in advance and quotations are adhered to.

The presentation of bills can help when they outline the benefits gained by the client for the fee being charged.

(a) Do the bills reflect the benefits gained by the client as well as the activity undertaken by the firm?
(b) What study does the firm undertake in relationship to quotations, expectation management and bill/fee presentation?

5.11 Follow-up

It is imperative that you follow up and stay in touch with past clients. The aim is for clients to see you as 'their solicitor'. It is the 'Holy Grail' but it cannot any longer be relied upon. It can however, be worked on. The saddest sentence uttered, after all this hard work is 'and, do you know, I never ever heard from them again'.

(a) What is your firm's system for following up with a satisfied client?
(b) How good is your firm at maintaining contact with your past satisfied clients?

6 Developing and using a professional contacts register (PCR)

What we term a professional contacts register (PCR) may be one of the most powerful tools any firm can have in securing and maintaining new clients. It does no harm either for existing clients to hear another professional speak highly of the firm they have chosen to act on their behalf.

Our proposal regarding the PCR is that the firm, as a whole, should undertake formally what most partners and fee earners have been doing in an ad hoc way.

It invites you to consider who, in the course of their work, could say to their clients, customers, patients, or congregation 'You should see a solicitor about this'. Your task is to get a reasonable percentage of them saying 'You should see [*name of your firm*] about this.'

Clearly, the development of a PCR is a departmental matter. The conveyancing department will have different recommenders from, for example, the family or commercial departments. In fact it can go beyond departments to matter types within the same department of a firm.

The PCR is, of course, a database but one which is people, not address, driven.

In **Annex 6A** you will find a list of categories that could form the basis of a PCR for your firm. It is not definitive and should be considered departmentally as there are bound to be categories relating to your firm that are not included. Smaller firms may decide to concentrate resources on a limited number of categories to start with, and this is exactly the right approach.

Annex 6B contains a draft letter to fee earning staff introducing the principle of the PCR to them, enlisting their help and explaining the PCR's importance. It is of course a draft and should be refined. The PCR development is important to the growth of your firm, and therefore to the security of employment of everyone in it.

The PCR register input questionnaire form in **Annex 6C** should be attached to the letter as drafted by you. It shows the categories of information required and will facilitate a consistent approach to data inputting.

Once your initial PCR has been produced, whether it is via reference to directories or reliant on the returns of fee earning staff, a programme of communications should be ready to be put in place.

One-off contact will rarely work, and this is why all professional marketeers will develop campaigns. You must too, and remember the purpose of the campaign is to persuade your professional contacts to recommend you to their contacts, at the appropriate time.

To do this you need to be presenting benefits, both for the work you can undertake, and for the PCR recommender, even if that is only kudos (no one is proposing referral fees or any other form of payment here). You need to be putting forward your message regularly (a campaign) and avoiding repetition and boredom with variety and innovation.

Annex 6D contains a programme of communications that has been proven to work and which you could adapt to your own requirements. Its aim is to produce meaningful and interesting contact with your PCR every two months.

Like much promotional activity there is a danger that this communication can fall foul of client needs. Taking time to prepare your programme of communications with the PCR, in advance, will greatly ease the pressure as deadlines approach. See **Annex 6E** for an example checklist.

Annex 6A
Professional contacts register category list

This list is by no mean exhaustive. Different departments within the firm, and indeed even different matter types, will have differing organisations who could, in the course of their work, recommend their clients, customers, patients, congregations, etc. to specific departments of the firm. Therefore, the following list should be looked upon simply as a guide.

Potential professional contacts register (PCR) members:

- Accountants
- Architects
- Banks (private and commercial)
- Building societies
- Care homes
- Charitable and voluntary organisations
- Churches
- Clinics (of all types)
- Commercial finance
- Day care centres
- Detective agencies
- Employment agencies
- Estate agents (domestic and commercial)
- Estate developers
- Expert witnesses
- Financial advisors
- Health authorities
- Hospitals
- Insolvency practitioners
- Insurance consultants
- Letting agents
- Life insurance consultants and companies
- Local government
- Loss adjusters
- Occupational health practitioners
- Pension consultants and companies
- Police stations
- Schools
- Social workers
- Surgeries
- Surveyors
- Therapists
- Trade associations
- Trade unions
- Undertakers

Annex 6B

Letter to fee earners encouraging development of the professional contacts register

Dear Colleague,

As part of our continuing practice development, we would like you to consider which of your contacts may say to their clients or customers, etc. 'You should see a solicitor about this'. These people comprise our professional contacts and we are putting together a register of them so that we can maintain contact with them on an automatic and regular basis.

Clearly each department will have a different group of contacts who could recommend our firm. Perhaps with your colleagues or departmental heads you could review the industry categories attached [as per Annex 6A] and consider who, in each relevant category, you already know.

Please remember that this database must be person, not address, driven.

Please also be as wide-ranging as you can in your thinking. Initially, we are looking for your contacts, but they do not necessarily have to be contacts who have already made recommendations to our firm. Perhaps for example, you would like to include your own bank manager.

Once everyone has returned their own contacts we will then compare these with published directories such as Yellow Pages to see what percentage of the potential we already command.

If appropriate we may then instigate a programme of developing contacts with people within important firms within our area who we do not know.

The intention is to develop a regular and automatic programme of communications with these people so that over time they may begin to think of [name of firm] as the first choice firm to recommend to people.

All material used in communications with the professional contacts register (PCR) will be presented to you in advance of its distribution.

If you have any queries regarding this please do contact me personally, but finally I would like to impress upon you the element of urgency there is in receiving your reply.

Best wishes,

[Senior partner]

Annex 6C
Professional contacts register input questionnaire form

Please note all contacts in the professional contacts register (PCR) must be listed by name first, not by organisation.

Name of contact (salutation, first name, surname):	
Name of organisation:	
Address including post code:	
Email:	
Type of introducer (e.g. bank, accountant, survey, estate agent, etc.):	
Main/principal contact in firm:	
Contact category:	
Last contact date:	
Action to be taken:	

Annex 6D
The professional contacts register usage and programme of communications

1 Initial letter

This should contain the following information:

- Who you are.
- What you do that is relevant to the person you are writing to.
- Who they should contact.
- Why you would be delighted to call in and meet them, visit them and tell them more about your practice.
- Or, that they are very welcome to come in and see you.
- Unless they tell you otherwise, even if you do not meet up, you will keep them on your mailing list and keep in touch.

2 First newsletter

This should be despatched with a personalised covering letter saying, for example, 'This newsletter is obviously produced in house for our clients, but I thought you might like a copy and would be interested in the article on page 3'.

Issue 1 of the newsletter and every subsequent issue should include one or more articles relevant to certain sections of the professional contacts register (PCR), for example, an article about the spring time upturn in property sales for estate agents, or pre-budget news for accountants, etc.

3 Literature kit

Assuming that you introduce the recommended literature kit in due course, one of its clear usages is to communicate with the PCR so that they understand you and your services more fully. A full kit in a folder, with a covering letter, should be mailed. This letter should be based upon the following:

> Please find enclosed our new literature kit. We are rather proud of this kit and hope that it will be of interest to you. We do not want to inundate you, but enclosed you will find half a dozen copies. If you need any more for your clients, or your staff, please do not hesitate to ask.

4 Website announcement

For example:

> We have just updated our website. It is well worth a look. You'll find it at [*website address*]. Why not log on and tell us what you think?

5   'What is a brand and why should you care?'

This should be a simple letter discussing your brand image and what it means.

6   'Planning ahead'

A letter with a dedicated publication for the elderly and their carers:

> Please find a copy of our latest publication 'Planning ahead'. You will see that this is to assist older clients and provide general advice for the elderly and their carers. If you would like additional copies for distribution to your staff or clients, please do not hesitate to ask.

7   Come to a round table lunch

An invitation to a round table lunch, for example:

> We think a general discussion between professionals can be of great use. We plan to hold such a lunch on [date] and hope that you will attend. Please contact me for more details.

8   Letters with news

The 'Planning ahead' publication above is a good illustration of matters that are of interest to particular sections of the PCR only. The departmental head should consider what areas of activity or initiatives he/she is planning, and ensure that part of that campaign includes a letter with news about the initiative for the appropriate section of the PCR.

10   [Name of firm] announces a client registration scheme

The client registration scheme is an important initiative that will not be emulated by a lot of people. Therefore it is likely to have an interest and impact in your own area. When producing the material relating to it, and introducing it to your existing client database, do not forget to tell the entire PCR. You are introducing something positive and free of charge to clients, which will have an impact and will increase the recommendations passed to you from the entire PCR.

11   'Look who we're sponsoring'

Make sure the whole PCR knows of any sponsorship that your firm undertakes. Include the PCR in letters that explain what you are doing and why, forward press releases to them, make sure they get copies of any press coverage you receive and generally involve them in activities.

Annex 6E

Using your professional contacts register checklist

- Date on which the professional contacts register (PCR) will be ready for use.
- Date on which the draft of the initial contact letter will be in place.
- Date of its despatch.
- Date and contents of subsequent follow-up letter.
- How will the newsletter be produced?
- Who will be responsible for its production?
- Distribution date of issue one.
- Contents list and distribution date of issue two.
- Outline article list and target distribution date for issue three.
- Date on which the literature kit production programme will in place.
- Date of first print run of literature kit.
- Proposed date for distribution of literature kit to the PCR.
- Date of website updating.
- Date of website announcement letter to the PCR.
- Is the elderly market a target?
- Will you proceed with a publication such as 'Planning ahead'?
- Who will be responsible for its creation and production?
- When will it be published?
- How will it be coordinated into an overall campaign with, for example, care homes?
- Are matrimonial and family matters an area for growth in the firm?

    - If so, are you going to proceed with a divorce helpline?
    - What publication will you use and what date of publication?
    - Following these decisions, what date will you announce the divorce helpline to the PCR?

- Is the firm going to run a client registration scheme?

    - If so, when will it be ready?
    - How will it be promoted initially to your client base?
    - How and when will it be announced to your PCR?

7 The three tiers of promotion

The 'three tiers of promotion' is a concept that differentiates the forms of promotion, and the purpose of them.

Broadly speaking, all promotional activity can be broken down into three areas:

* Corporate (image) promotion.
* Product-specific promotion.
* Market-specific promotion.

7.1 Corporate (image) promotion

All corporate image promotion is organised to ensure that all past clients, existing and current clients, prospects and professional contacts know where your firm is, what it does, how to contact it, and wherever possible includes an indication of your firm's 'profile' or ethos. (This is discussed further in **Chapter 8**.) A clear understanding of a firm's brand is of particular importance when undertaking corporate image style promotion.

Dependent upon the type of promotion and the media selected, corporate image promotion may include (in addition to the presentation of brand and ethos) a background to the firm, a client charter, a list of services, maps and methods of contacting the firm and the promotion of your website as a source of additional information.

7.2 Product-specific promotion

This is a form of promotion where the firm, or a department within the firm, takes a specific product, service or package of services and promotes it along with its specific benefits to all prospective and existing clients and the PCR. (This is a good illustration of 'horizontal' expansion discussed in **Chapter 5**.)

Each department has a range of products including its 'prime products' and a resource capacity for increasing the volume of work in this area. These are the products that should be promoted.

When a specific matter type such as conveyancing is being promoted, clearly the details of that product and its benefits need to be included in the promotional activity. The promotion will probably be geared to a 'call to action' that involves either direct contact with the firm, or reference to the website where more detail of the benefits and elaborate explanations are provided. There is also the opportunity within product promotion for linking a central product with other associated products (a will with an LPA for example) and the opportunity for providing both product extension and differentiation. An extension of a product can include additional extra services, such as home visits, which can also assist in differentiating your product from other similar products.

7.3 Market-specific promotion

This is an activity where a specific market or market niche has been defined and a full range of appropriate services have been brought together for clients within that niche.

An obvious market in this category is the high profile, relatively wealthy and continually growing elderly client market. It is no coincidence that this is a market that is being deliberately targeted by the 'new competition' (we discuss an approach to the 'elderly market' in more detail in **Chapter 13**).

When a specific market such as the elderly is being tackled, the firm's promotion needs to demonstrate its understanding, experience and ability to handle all aspects of that market. This activity may include such things as larger fonts on that section of the website, specifically written inserts for the literature kit, a detailed publication, seminars, home visits, etc.

Annex 7A
Three tiers of promotion checklist

Corporate (image) promotion

- What corporate image promotion has the firm undertaken in the past?
- What information on the firm did it include?
- What attempt was made at presenting the firm's 'brand' or 'ethos'?
- How was it measured?
- How successful was it?
- What corporate image promotion is currently being undertaken?
- How is it being measured?
- What 'call to action' is included in this promotion?
- How will it be deemed successful or otherwise?
- What future corporate image promotion is being considered?
- What corporate image promotion was considered in the past but rejected?
- Why was it rejected?

Product-specific promotion

- Which departments have 'product promotions' running?
- How is success being measured?
- Is the promotion benefit based?
- What other products of the firm could be promoted?
- How?
- Why has this promotion (or something like it) not happened yet?

Market-specific promotion

- Has the firm ever undertaken market-specific promotional activity?
- What was this activity?
- How successful was it?
- What market-specific promotional activity is currently being undertaken by the firm?
- What are the products or groups of products being presented in each market niche case?
- How are they being measured?
- Do they look like they are being successful?
- What other market or niche promotion should be considered for the future?

8 Your firm's brand

'Branding' does not have to be a logo, catchphrase or any other 'corporate image' presentation, although it can incorporate all these things and others. Rather, 'branding' is first a recognition of what the firm is and does, its own uniqueness, its position in the market place, the range of services it provides, which segment of the market it provides to, and how it stands in competition with both the traditional and new providers of legal services.

Of course, in part this is a recognition of the benefits your firm has to offer its clients, which is why **Chapter 1** of this toolkit is so important, but it is more than this. It includes an understanding of what it is the outside world thinks of when it hears your firm's name. There needs to be an understanding of what people actually think, as a starting point to persuading them to see your practice as you think it is, or would like it to be.

Of course, the 'product' range you offer and the geographical market you serve are part of your brand. So, of course, are the benefits to be derived from the purchase of these 'products' by that market. But it is also more than that.

Consider the following:

- Are you a market leader or a follower?
- Are you a high-price provider, mid-price player or volume-driven discount organisation?
- Is your service aimed at private clients only? Or company/commercial? Or are you a full service provider? Or, as in the case of most 'high street' firms, mainly private client with a little (mostly property/employment) work for the owner/driver/businessman?
- Is your firm old fashioned/traditional/forward thinking/'trendy'?
- Are fee earners/partners predominately older/younger/a good mix of ages?
- Are fee earners/partners predominately male/female/a good mix between genders?
- Are you a city/town/county practice?
- What are the market segments/niches that your firm currently serves?
- What are some additional segments/niches that your firm would like to serve in the future?

An important part of developing your brand is being able to differentiate between reality and perception. There is a balance to be drawn. Where perception outreaches reality there is a danger of dissatisfied clients, and a need for expectation management. Where reality exceeds perception there is a danger that the firm will not be used or recommended and a clear brand definition and benefit presentation is needed.

By gradually building on the list indicated above, and utilising the benefit analysis, you will begin to define your firm's 'profile'. It is a fact that like attracts like, and therefore that your profile will appeal to those with similar profiles. To be attracted to you, these potential clients need to recognise the similarities and understand them. Your task is to project this brand image and this is what branding is all about.

To take two examples, anyone exposed to the brands of Coca-Cola or Halifax Legal Express immediately understands what these brands stand for, what these companies provide, how they will be handled/treated and the benefits they will derive from the product/services.

Fortunately you do not need to have the worldwide recognition of Coca-Cola or the national recognition that Halifax is achieving.

What you do need, is to be as clearly understood in your own geographical area or market segment as these firms are in theirs.

Halifax is being used here as an example of the 'new competition'. As mentioned in **Chapter 9**, there is much to be learned from reviewing the websites of this 'new competition'.

While making the recommended review it is important to remember the 'new competition' do not have any secret tricks or magic formulae that they use to win business. It is a fact that your firm could be as big in your own chosen market.

In developing your own brand and considering the facets of your firm that make up your brand, it is worth considering the brand assets of the 'new competition' in comparison with a traditional legal practice such as your own.

A simple comparison of these brand assets illustrates the important point that the traditional firm can do much in their own geographical area than the 'new competition' do nationally and that you have many brand assets that they cannot deploy.

8.1 The new competition: brand assets

8.1.1 Customer focused

Most of these firms are marketing-led. They understand clients' needs, and how to demonstrate that the benefits they offer can service those needs.

The message of this toolkit is that you too must take this attitude and learn from the competition.

8.1.2 Multi-channel communications

Apart from the obvious and expensive level of advertising and direct mail, the 'new competition' are very adept at utilising the internet and social media. Ways to utilise these methods are discussed in **Chapter 9**.

8.1.3 Multi-million pound budgets

But why do you need these? You are dealing in a limited geographical area basing an approach upon existing satisfied clients and recommenders. You have to recognise that your client base is being 'attacked' and you need to defend it but it does not need to cost millions.

8.1.4 Brand value

There are recognisable names and 'profiles' superimposed upon the provision of legal services. But you can do this too, and you are a solicitor.

8.1.5 Millions of customers

This would be a customer base that most firms neither need nor could service.

8.2 The traditional firm: brand assets

8.2.1 Learning from competition

This is the ability to understand the 'new competition' and present against it.

8.2.2 Legal expertise

You are a solicitor, this is what you do, and everyone understands that.

8.2.3 The Law Society and SRA

Everyone recognises that solicitors are controlled and regulated by their governing bodies, while, incorrectly, the perception of the 'new competition' is that they are not.

The Law Society as the representative body for solicitors has a range of resources designed to help you to market your firm. See **Appendix A** for details of Law Society accreditation schemes; and **Appendix B** for a list of relevant publications. For full details of how the Law Society can help your firm, see the website at **www. lawsociety.org.uk**

8.2.4 Past satisfied clients

As noted in **Chapter 4** your client database is your seedcorn. While this is true of the 'new competition', your database knows you already for the provision of legal services. The 'new competition' is known to their customers for a plethora of other products (this should not be taken as an underestimation of the power of their brand).

8.2.5 Nearby offices

This is an extremely important additional benefit of your brand. With commitment and dedication, your firm could offer all the 24/7 availability and interactivity of the 'new competition' while in addition providing 'pop-in ability'. Do not underestimate this.

8.2.6 Local links and contacts

Local links and contacts are also important: you know your own area in a way that none of the 'new competition' or other centrally based providers can. Local links mean you know your area and people working there, and its likely developments. Local contacts enable you to work with people you know, and, with a little effort, actively seek recommendation. The 'new competition' can do none of this.

8.2.7 Local recognition

Many firms have operated in the same location for decades and, as a result, are recognised for what they do and who they are. This can be developed in a way impossible to 'outsiders'.

8.2.8 Surveys

Despite the effort and money poured into the legal market place by the 'new competition', every meaningful survey over the last two years has indicated that the general public not only want to see the continuation and success of an independent legal profession, but put a solicitor as their first port of call for legal services. This is very strong knowledge to play on in your branding, but it also indicates that the profession may be losing out to those 'enquirers' who do not buy their legal services from that 'first port of call'.

8.3 You must develop your own brand

The aim of your brand must be to:

- create awareness in your defined market;
- acquire new clients at the expense of your traditional and new competitors;
- retain clients.

A brand can assist you in the ultimate aim of creating a situation where all of your past satisfied clients consider you to be 'their solicitor' whom they approach/ recommend automatically and exclusively when their own, or other people's needs for legal services arise.

Your firm's brand should be developed specifically to serve the understanding of your chosen client group, in your defined geographical area, around the full range of services you have to offer and their benefits.

8.4 Brand development is constant communication

Some of the tools for regular communication are discussed in this toolkit. They include:

- a benefit-based literature kit (see **Chapter 11**);
- regular and informative newsletters (see **Chapter 10**);
- letters with news in/e-shots (see **Chapter 10**);
- website and social media (see **Chapter 9**);
- press releases (see **14.2**);
- seminars and sponsorship (see **Chapter 14**);
- product promotion (see **Chapter 7**);
- client registration scheme (see **Chapter 12**);
- professional contacts register (see **Chapter 6**).

Annex 8A
Developing your own brand

To develop and understand your brand you need to consider the following. (This is not an exhaustive list.)

- What is the range of services offered to private clients?
- What is the range of services offered to commercial clients?
- What publicly-funded work does the firm undertake?
- What market niches does the firm serve?
- What special qualifications or experience does the firm have within its fee earning staff (e.g. maritime law, intellectual property rights)?
- What special attributes can members of the firm offer (e.g. foreign language speakers)?
- What is the geographical market the firm serves (this does not of course preclude taking work from it, but is likely to your main target for promotion)?
- Would you describe your firm as a market leader or follower?
- Is your firm a high-price provider, a mid-price price player or a volume-driven discount organisation?
- Would you describe your firm as old fashioned, traditional, forward thinking or 'trendy'?
- Are the fee earners/partners predominantly older/younger/a good mix of ages?
- Are fee earners/partners predominantly male/female/a good mix of genders?
- Are you a city/town/county practice?
- How would you describe your typical private client?
- How would you define your most important area of commercial work?
- Who is your most important commercial client?
- Assuming your existing client base represents the firm's brand as it was/is now, does it also represent how you see your firm in the future?
- What changes would you make to enhance your firm's image and brand?

9 Your website and marketing using social media

In this chapter we look at websites and the internet. Perhaps nothing has changed or developed as fast in the last five years as the way the internet has become inextricably linked with the promotion and execution of legal work.

There can be no doubt that this development has been led by the 'new competition' who all have extremely good websites. These websites are a lesson to all in the profession (outside the major national/multinational city firms who, like the 'new competition', have marketing departments and excellent websites). These sites are easy to navigate, clear, interactive in many cases and provide legal advice and access to solicitors at all times.

These sites set the standard of providing legal services in terms of benefits derived by the clients rather than procedures or rules and almost always speak in the language of the client, rather than that of the profession.

Our strongest advice is to make a study of the 'new competition' sites and learn from them. You will find assistance to do this in **Annex 9A**. As you will see from the exercise, it is also relevant to make a study of the national firms referred to above. Perhaps this does not seem relevant to you, but there is much to learn and some very good ideas to be obtained for this study. However, we also recommend a systematic review of your traditional, local, competitor solicitors.

Another relatively recent innovation that you should be aware of is the extraordinary increase in the advent and proliferation of legal work seeking websites, comparison sites and apparent advisors. These go much further than the traditional 'claims farmers' as they were called and our most recent survey found no fewer than 50 separate sites that effectively stand between you and your prospective clients, while actively promoting themselves in competition to you to your existing client base.

When you are making this website review consider whether the website is:

- professional;
- friendly;
- efficient;
- interesting;
- uncluttered;
- easy to navigate;
- benefit-based;
- market-specific (by section).

Now, using the same criteria, review your own existing website and consider whether or not it is due for revamping and updating.

Of all the above list, 'ease of navigation' is probably the most important. You know your site, so get a trusted outsider to review it cold and report back.

Remember, one of the basic facts of websites is that your competitors are just one or two clicks away from your own website.

Again, when you review, carefully consider the copy and graphics that are being used. Few words, lots of space, nice graphics, and a specific call to action are the key.

Increasingly, you will find how important interactivity has become, and how its importance is still growing (see **9.5**).

It is not the role of a toolkit such as this to discuss website design or designers, except to say that your research will undoubtedly illustrate the wide range in quality, content and usability demonstrated by similar sites that have cost similar amounts.

On this subject we have but two pieces of advice:

(a) Carefully select a professional website designer with whom you have a good rapport and who understands both the profession and your firm's ethos and brand.
(b) Brief the designer fully and clearly and then let the designer do the rest. Your research will demonstrate clearly to you those sites that have been designed by a 'committee' and we all know what happened to the racehorse designed by a committee.

One of the biggest problems with websites is that many areas of content can quickly go out-of-date, e.g. through law changes or changes within a firm. Sometimes, the product range will change and continually the operating environment varies.

Just as it is important to have a structure for the technical maintenance for computer hardware and software, it is also extremely important that content and advice are both current and, of course, accurate. Someone in your firm must be appointed to manage this vital area.

Of equal importance is how firms respond to enquiries created by the website. Clearly, this is a matter for individual firms to deal with, but the problem with instant access is that instant response is expected. Within the context of this advice, it is worth considering who is viewing your site. Generally they will be visitors who have found you by chance or through recommendation: people who are already considering instructing your firm but are 'checking you out'. Other visitors will be competitors seeing what you are doing, browsers and prospective employees.

Your web designer and host will be able to advise on website report usage but it is a matter of this information's interpretation that will result in making your site more efficient.

Your site on its own is not the salvation of your marketing ambitions. It too needs promoting. You can promote the site itself in literature kits, newsletters and in other correspondence, including in your letterhead. Your technical advisors will advise on search engine optimisation, metatags, Google Adwords and other technical promoters, but above all there is a need, as always, to promote benefits: in this case the benefit of viewing your site.

What exactly will users gain from visiting your site? What is in it for them? Why should they put you on their list of sites to be viewed?

9.1 Enquiry volumes

Quality and quantity of enquiries present an additional aspect to the website promotion. If you launch a website that offers a popular service at a special price and you are inundated with enquiries, will you be able to handle them? Promoting your website needs to balance the number of enquiries you need to keep the department running profitably while not generating too many and disappointing potential clients.

Before promoting your site consider the following points:

* How many enquiries do you want?
* What level of quality of enquiries do you expect?
* How many new matters do you need to generate from website enquiries?
* What flexibility do you need in enquiry numbers?

9.2 Your role in the promotion of your site

The first stage is to realise that you cannot leave your website 'floating in cyberspace'. You must actively promote it yourself and be sure that your promotional activity is successful with clients, prospects and your professional contacts.

9.2.1 Promotion: the benefits of being a website viewer

The starting point for persuading a prospect or past client to view the site is to explain to them the benefits of doing so. These could include:

* a registered client may gain access to valuable restricted information;
* your past clients will have easy access to your firm's information;
* prospects will get an impression of your firm's services and benefits;

- professional contacts register (PCR) members can access support and information before recommending the firm.

If your firm is departmentalised, even if the same section of your firm is servicing different market niches, there is a need to consider both the content and the advantages of viewing from a 'departmental' point of view.

9.2.2 Encourage visits to your site

The onus is on you to encourage visitors to your site. Visitors who come by chance are a bonus. This initial promotion should be via word of mouth, and fee earners and support staff should be encouraged to promote the website, pointing out its benefits, in their conversations with clients, prospects, professional contacts and even socially.

In addition you need to direct everyone towards your website via your letter head, business cards and literature.

Your literature kit should have a website-dedicated insert explaining to the recipient why they should use the website. This is one of the few inserts that should go out with every literature kit. (See **Chapter 11**.)

Use your directory advertising (e.g. Yellow Pages) to promote the website alongside the telephone number of your firm.

All your generic advertising and PR activity should include promotion of the website along with any social media activity.

9.3 Social media

The ever-increasing amount of traffic on social media sites indicates the necessity for your firm to consider promoting its e-services, not only through your website, but on other web resources such as social media sites.

Social media sites and services include:

- Facebook;
- MySpace;
- LinkedIn;
- Twitter;
- Vimeo;
- Xing;
- other blogging, website and discussion groups.

Your firm needs to understand the value of social media, and its potential growth in the very near future, and devise a firm-wide policy relating to its usage and the promotion of the firm thereon.

The best users of social networks integrate the networks into their daily communication systems. For example anything that is published, either in print form or on the website, should also automatically be fed into these social networks. There is no harm in a story or promotional piece being seen in different media. Indeed this is precisely what a 'campaign' is.

The Law Society has published a detailed practice note on social media which gives guidance as to how to set up a social media policy and areas to look out for. It can be found at **www.lawsociety.org.uk/advice/practice-notes/social-media**

For an example social media policy, see **Annex 9D**.

9.4 Developing and improving your website

The tasks related to developing and improving your website can be split into three areas of executive responsibility:

- *Development:* using the approach outlined in this chapter, develop a framework for assessing and improving your own firm's website based on the research recommended in **Annex 9A**.
- *Management:* there is a need to appoint someone to be responsible for the delivery of the firm's internet and website services. This is one of the areas where a 'committee' might perform best. It is possible that the senior management have a clear view of the firm's strategy but a younger member of the team may be more up-to-date or au fait with the latest development in hardware, software and indeed internet/social media usage.
- *Promotion:* your website is a portal to your firm in the same way that your reception area is. Therefore, it also needs continual promotion to ensure traffic comes 'through the door'.

9.5 Website interactivity

Too often the creation of a new website is seen as the end of a long development process. It is not. It is the beginning of a sales process that will only have any value if it is handled well, responded to and indeed promoted. It is important to make sure your website is being utilised to its full sales capability.

You need to research and consider the five ways that visitors can respond to your website:

1. *No response.* You need to record the number of visitors to your site that result in no action.
2. *Email.* The internal system within your firm must ensure that your response to this email is almost immediate.
3. *Telephone.* The best sites will expend a considerable amount of space and use enlarged text to promote their telephone number, and encourage people to use it. Your response staff need to be trained in how to handle enquiries that are frequently more informed as a result of having come from the website.

4. *Downloading information.* Were potential clients to request information by post they would have to provide their name and address. If people are able to download a PDF version of your literature kit, for example, then perhaps they should also indicate who they are by providing their email address before being able to do so.

5. *Document assembly.* In more advanced systems, notably within the 'new competition', there is document assembly, or automation technology. This generates employment contracts and wills using templates online. This can turn a browser into a paying client.

Annex 9A

Website research and development list

List five (or more) local traditional solicitors who are competitors of your firm and make comparisons between their websites and your own:

1.
2.
3.
4.
5.

List five (or more) regional or national solicitors firms for a comparison of their websites and a trawl for ideas:

1.
2.
3.
4.
5.

Research alternative legal service providers (the 'new competition') in addition to those you have already listed:

* Halifax Legal Express – **www.halifaxlegalexpress.co.uk**
* NatWest Mentor – **www.natwestmentor.co.uk/services**
* Saga Legal Services – **www.sagalegalservices.co.uk**
* Automobile Association – **www.theaa.com**
* The Co-operative Society Legal Services – **www.co-operative.coop/legalservices**

It is important that you make your own consideration of the 'new competition' related to your geographic market and the services you provide. A simple Google search will provide an astounding number of people purporting to provide or advise on legal services in competition to you.

For each of the websites you choose, make a note of/print the pages that indicate what you like about that website. Note the methods of navigation around the website and how the menus of services and information work. Also, include illustrations of what you do not like or things you do not want in your own website. Collate the notes and pages into a rough style guide for your website.

Use the suggested list of qualities below to assess the site. Note: you may want to add categories that are specific to your firm or the services it provides.

* Good first impressions
* Professional
* Friendly
* Efficient

- Interesting
- Uncluttered
- Easy to navigate
- Benefit based
- Market-specific

Interactivity

Below is a list of common types of interactivity. Consider how these will generate enquiries by easily allowing the viewer to contact your firm. Then consider those that are helpful to your own practice.

- Email contact forms
- Helpful downloads
- Telephone call back services
- Quotations – automated or manual
- Appointment booking
- Text messages (SMS)
- Pre-appointment information gathering questionnaire/form

Annex 9B

Example website map

It is important to ensure that the content of your website integrates with your current promotional campaigns. The regular updating of your site, particularly its news pages, its blog and its archiving (for example of your newsletter) is essential.

The following is a very brief outline of a website map, which may help in developing your own website, following comparison with other sites [*as outlined in Annex 9A*].

Home page

- Our team
- How to find us/contact us

Corporate

- Dispute resolution and litigation
- Finance
- Human resources
- Property and conveyancing
- Tax
- Technology and commerce
- Industrial and commercial expertise
- Employment law
- Litigation, contracts and agreements

Private client

Wills

- Single parent wills
- Husband and wife mirror wills
- Separated spouses
- Cross life interest wills
- Flexible life interest trusts
- Wills for co-habitants

Estate and tax planning

- Inheritance tax
- Capital Gains Tax
- Tax planning through trusts

Enduring powers of attorney

- Creation
- Registration
- Management of affairs
- (Lasting) powers of attorney
- Court of Protection

Probate and administration of estates

- Receivership applications, accounts, general directions
- Administering of estates, obtaining a grant of representation
- Full administration and inheritance/income tax
- Elderly client
- Long-term care funding
- Deeds of gift
- Trusts
- Savings trusts
- Protection of assets

About us

- History of the firm
- Our partners
- Our team
- Partner profiles
- Publications and events
- Newsletter archiving
- Useful information
- Hot topics
- Links to other websites
- Community
- Pro bono, charities
- Our technology
- E-business services
- E-client services
- Careers with us
- Lawyers support and secretarial staff graduates
- Contact us

While the above list is fine, there is a real danger that it could be written as a series of procedural activities. It is absolutely vital when writing website copy that the benefits of obtaining each service be clearly illustrated in understandable language, and that you do not shy away from introducing the idea of how dangerous it would be to not have the work done satisfactorily.

At the end of each section, perhaps even at the end of each page, there should be a call to action and a way of executing that action such as 'email us now' with a click on email contact or 'telephone us now' with a large freephone number.

Annex 9C

Website management policy

1   Person with overall responsibility

1.1   The person with overall responsibility for the [*name of firm*] website(s) is [*name and job title*].

1.2   [His/her] responsibilities include [*list of responsibilities and decision-making powers. You may also wish to exclude certain powers, for example, budget authorisation above a certain level. If so, how these decisions will be taken could be included in the policy*].

2   Our website

[*Set out the business objectives and plans for your website. A simple statement of the practice's objectives in relation to the site, how it will achieve them and how it plans to develop the site will help to clarify these matters and ensure that they are communicated throughout the practice. This section could include a general statement about the practice's approach to management of the site – a tight, centrally-controlled approach or one which allows content owners more autonomy.*]

3   Website management

3.1   Day-to-day operational control questions, including security matters, should be addressed to [*name or function/job title and contact details*].

3.2   Other roles include [*list roles. If you have a large site with many different roles and responsibilities you may wish to set these out in a table along with contact details. Alternatively you may wish to simply put the principal contact in your policy and set out other roles and responsibilities in a separate document. This section should be distinguished from section 4 where key roles in relation to document approval and publishing should be identified.*]

4   Document approval and publishing

4.1   Final responsibility for approving new or revised documents for publication on the website rests with [*name(s) and role(s)*].

4.2   In this context 'document' includes [*list of types of publication that are subject to the approval and publication process*] and excludes [*for example, blogs, etc.*].

4.3   Before publication is approved they [*or you if this is delegated to content owners*] will need to be satisfied that the document meets the required standards in the following areas:

    4.3.1   Compliance: [*set out standards of compliance and person responsible for sign-off*]

    4.3.2   Quality: [*set out standards of quality and person responsible for sign-off*]

    4.3.3   Conformance: [*set out standards of conformance and person responsible for sign-off*]

4.4   They will also need to be satisfied that a review period or expiry date has been set.

5 Permitted and prohibited use

[*This section is most appropriate for setting out the limits of any delegated authority to update the content of the site, rather than regulatory compliance. How you intend to comply with, for example, the Electronic Commerce Directive can either be dealt with in section 4.3 above – by identifying the person required to sign-off a document – or in a separate document. The latter option is probably best.*]

6 Security and content management

6.1   Website security forms part of our overall information security policy which can be found at [*location of policy*].

6.2   Resources for guidance, training and support in information security, including website security, are available to all staff at [*location of guidance, etc.*]. Please contact [*name/role and contact details*] for help and advice. To report a security incident please contact [*name/role and contact details*] or in an emergency or after business hours contact [*name/role and contact details*].

7 Annual review

7.1   This policy will be reviewed annually on [*date*] by [*name of relevant member in senior management team*] as part of the annual review of the information management system.

7.2   If you have any suggestions for how this policy could be improved please contact [*name and contact details of relevant member in senior management team or delegate*].

Annex 9D
Social media policy

Social media is web-based and mobile technology that turns communication into interactive dialogue. This includes Facebook, LinkedIn and Twitter but there are many more websites, blogs and internet forums that allow dialogue across a web-based platform and these are all subject to this policy.

[If the practice has no wish to use social media]

[*Name of firm*] does not use social media in its marketing or communications. The use of social media is prohibited during work time and on [*name of firm*]'s computer equipment.

Any information or comments posted on social media sites outside work time must not include any reference to the practice or any [partners/members/directors], employees or clients of the practice, must not bring the practice into disrepute and must not breach the SRA Code of Conduct 2011. Particular regard must be had to the solicitor's duty of confidentiality under Chapter 4 of the Code.

[*Name*] will be responsible for [*name of firm*]'s social media use and will review the policy annually.

[If the firm uses social media in a more active way]

This firm has a presence on [*name of website(s), e.g. Facebook, LinkedIn, Twitter*]. This is managed by [*name*] and no other person is authorised to update the practice's presence on these sites without the agreement of a [partner/member/director].

Any information or comments posted on these sites by any [partner/member/director] or employee of the practice must not in any way bring the practice into disrepute, must comply with the SRA Code of Conduct 2011 and must not include any confidential information about the practice or its clients. Employees should make certain before posting any information that it reflects the standards and policies of the practice. Under no circumstances should information or comments of a confidential or sensitive nature be posted on the internet.

Information posted or viewed on a social media site may constitute published material. Therefore, reproduction of information posted or otherwise available over the internet may be done only with the express permission of the copyright holder. Employees must not act in such a way as to breach copyright or the licensing conditions of any website or computer program.

[Partners/Directors/Members] and employees of [*name of firm*] are encouraged to have their own profile on business-based social media sites (e.g. LinkedIn) so long as the above guidance is complied with and [*name of person responsible for maintaining the practice's social media presence*] is aware of and has access to that profile.

Any breach of this policy will be considered a disciplinary matter to be dealt with through the practice's disciplinary procedures.

10 How newsletters can work for your firm

Chapter 8 discussed your firm's 'brand' and the need to promote it through regular communications with all interested parties, be they past satisfied clients, prospects or the PCR.

This chapter begins that process by looking at the use of newsletters and how they can work for you. To be clear, when we are speaking of newsletters it is the entity we are referring to. The delivery may be print and post, email, e-shots or event leaflet drop, including distribution at reception and, perhaps, at seminars. We have already indicated that promotional material should also be distributed automatically via various social media, but it is the content more than the media we are concerned with here.

10.1 The value of a newsletter

- It can help you prosper in a competitive market by continually presenting the benefits you have to offer to clients, prospects and the contacts on your PCR.
- It is possibly the best vehicle to regularly present these benefits and then make comparisons with alternative suppliers.
- It can, in itself, demonstrate a proactive approach to client contact that is not traditional in your market.
- Promotion can seem to be repetitive. A newsletter allows you to tell similar 'stories' in different ways.
- It can give a human and approachable face to your practice that can help overcome some of the in-built, historical resistance that exists even today. This negative perception of solicitors is what is pushing clients towards 'new competition', therefore it is important to show the reality of dealing with your firm.

10.2 Get it right and you will gain enormously

Newsletters have in some small way fallen into disrepute and this is largely down to the laziness of the producers. If everyone is 'too busy' – don't do it. If you are simply going to buy in a newsletter and stamp your name on it – don't bother, your readers will soon see through it and can usually get the information you offer elsewhere anyway.

It must be your newsletter and that means writing it in-house, or having it written for your exclusive use. You have a great opportunity to be original because you are only aiming at a relatively small readership in a clearly defined area. You can be writing about local stories and issues.

10.3 Points to consider at the beginning

Your firm may already be producing a newsletter; if so, that newsletter should be used as the basis for development and hopefully some of the ideas listed here will be helpful.

However, this section of the toolkit is intended to assist and encourage readers to begin a series of newsletters for themselves.

1. Will your newsletter be general (for everyone) or specific (to a section of your client base such as elderly clients or commercial clients)?
2. If specific, then which section is the newsletter primarily aimed at?
3. Who else might be interested in this newsletter (e.g. which section of the PCR)?
4. How many issues a year are planned?
5. Who will produce the article list?
6. Which graphic designer/printer will you use?
7. What size will the newsletter be – A4, A3 folded, A5? How many pages? What type of binding will you use?
8. What type of style will the newsletter have (e.g. newspaper style, letter style or brochure style)?
9. How will the newsletter be distributed (e.g. post, DX, email, by hand, etc.)?

Once it has been decided to produce a series of newsletters the following need to be considered.

10.4 Producing the newsletter

10.4.1 Layout and style

While the layout and style depend upon the market being addressed, it is important that a house style be adopted and presented consistently. It is essential to include colour photographs, and other graphics. New printing techniques have made this perfectly affordable and economically viable.

Generally speaking an A3 sheet folded once to produce an A4, four-page newsletter seems to be the most popular. However, this is of course not mandatory.

10.4.2 Copywriting

Copywriting is a skill, but solicitors are used to using words and many are capable of producing good newsletter copy. Should your firm not include someone capable of undertaking this task, your printer or graphic designer will no doubt be able to introduce you to a professional copywriter.

The copy need to be informative, but not too dry; friendly, but not over familiar; relevant without being boring; consistent without being repetitive.

10.4.3 Graphics and illustrations

It is important to break up blocks of text with graphics and illustrations. Because you are trying to put a human face into the equation, do not be afraid of using photographs, even informal ones.

10.4.4 The need for a series

There is little point in a one-off newsletter, unless it is for a specific and clearly defined purpose. For a newsletter to be meaningful and achieve the objectives set for it, it needs to be part of a series so that the recipients expect it, welcome it and learn from it. A popular frequency for newsletters is three issues a year.

10.4.5 Maintaining quality

Your copywriting, graphics, layout and printing will have already established a level of quality. Generally speaking the first issue is always of the highest quality, but the quality should not be allowed to slip. The simplest way of ensuring this is to have a fair proportion of the newsletter written well in advance. Of course space must be left for topical material but, as a rule of thumb, by the time the first issue is distributed the second issue should be at first draft stage and an article list (content list) prepared for the third issue.

10.4.6 Provision of information

Despite its informal and friendly approach, your newsletter must not neglect the provision of information relevant to the reader, and of course the presentation of your firm's benefits. This should be one of the criteria against which you measure your newsletter.

10.4.7 Standard 'standby' articles

It is a good plan to write a 'library' of standard articles that can be used in future editions to assist in maintaining quality and frequency. Clearly these articles need to be both generic and non-time specific.

10.4.8 'Topical' articles

By contrast, space needs to be left in the layout for each article to ensure the ability to introduce current and topical matters.

10.4.9 Linking your newsletter to your other campaigns

As noted above, your newsletter distribution may take place at events such as seminars, or even at social functions. However, there is an important role for the newsletter to play in the integrated campaigns themselves.

An integrated campaign is one where the same message is targeted at the same market segment via different routes and media.

As an illustration you may have decided to promote your conveyancing services to local estate agents, via different promotional activities, prior to the likely upturn in the housing market at spring time. In addition to the other initiatives you have planned, appropriate article(s) should be included in your newsletter. These articles must be of genuine interest to your usual readers (clients) but might be about your firm's close working relationship with other professionals in the property market, and how you set out to help rather than hinder any transaction, to everyone's obvious benefit.

Perhaps you have been promoting yourself to care homes as a specialist, with an interest in working for that home and providing services and even seminars to the residents. An article about care home fees, or your willingness to make home visits can reinforce your activity.

Doubtless accountants will be an important part of your PCR, especially if you undertake any company and commercial work. An article on directors' responsibilities, or the latest changes in employment law might be appropriate.

10.4.10 Proofreading

Any writer will tell you that a proofreader is essential. Mistakes that will be absolutely obvious to a first time reader are missed.

The final proofreading therefore should be undertaken by a first time reader, being someone who has not seen the articles before or been involved in their creation.

10.4.11 Post and PDF

Your newsletter artwork should be produced so that material can be printed, (probably in-house by your laser printer) prior to distribution via post, etc., but also made available as a PDF for downloading from your website.

A series of emails alerting people to the fact that your latest newsletter is available in PDF form can pay dividends, especially with the PCR.

10.4.12 Covering letter

Clearly your newsletter is written primarily for your clients. However, the inclusion of relevant articles for the different sections of the PCR in various issues can be extremely beneficial. When a newsletter is sent to a member of the PCR it should include a covering letter directing them to the specific article. It is interesting to note that once they have read that article, they will probably read the rest of the newsletter as well. See **Annex 10B** for an example of the type of letter that can be sent.

10.4.13   Archiving on your website

Each issue of your newsletter should be archived on your website to enable it to build into an interesting library of material that is available at any time in the future.

10.4.14   Monitoring feedback

It is likely that you will receive reader feedback to your newsletters, especially the early issues. It is important that a system is set up within your organisation to ensure that this feedback is monitored. This is not only for fine-tuning the style and content of the newsletter, but also to ensure a response is given to the reader who has taken time to write. Remember the newsletter is only part of an overall client communication strategy.

Annex 10A
Newsletter checklist

- What is the layout and style of the newsletter series to be?
- What is the title to be?
- What is the house style to be?
- Who will undertake the copyrighting and the collation of articles?
- What graphics and illustrations will be used in the first three issues?
- How will you ensure that you maintain quality?
- What articles do you have in your 'stand by' library?
- What topical articles should be included in the next issue?
- Who is going to undertake proofreading the newsletter?
- Which articles will be used to link in with other campaigns in the next three issues?
- Who will be responsible for managing distribution via post and PDF?
- Who will be responsible for archiving the newsletter on the website?
- Who will be responsible for monitoring feedback from the newsletter?

Annex 10B
Covering letter for newsletter

Dear [*name*]

I thought you might be interested in the enclosed newsletter.

As you can see our newsletter is produced in-house for our clients, but I hope you will find it of interest.

I felt that the articles on pages 2 and 4 would be particularly relevant to you.

I hope you will not hesitate to contact me should you wish to discuss anything about the article, and in any case I will as usual be in contact with you within the next couple of weeks.

Kind regards

[*Signed by the fee earner closest to the recipient*]

Annex 10C
Illustrative newsletter article template

Note: It is important to ensure that the introductory article, news about the firm, services promotion and good news stories are always included in each issue. However, it is important to ring the changes relating to the coverage for different departments, ensuring that each gets a turn to coincide with its promotional initiative.

Not all articles need attributing – but all should have some form of a 'call to action' and a contact point.

	Current issue (date)	Next issue (date)	Following issue (target date)
Introductory article [*This article, frequently attributed to a senior partner, is an introduction to the current issue, a résumé of the issue's contents, and a comment on the most relevant recent developments in the firm or the legal environment.*]			
In whose name?			
First draft received/date:			
Corrections made/date:			
Final copy approved/date:			
Sent to layout house/date:			
Private client department			
Article: [*e.g. Planning ahead for comfortable later life (care homes)*]			
In whose name?			
First draft received/date:			
Corrections made/date:			
Final copy approved/date:			
Sent to layout house/date:			
Article: [*e.g. Inheritance tax, care home costs and you (care homes)*]			
In whose name?			
First draft received/date:			

	Current issue (date)	Next issue (date)	Following issue (target date)
Corrections made/date:			
Final copy approved/date:			
Sent to layout house/date:			
Family department			
Article: [*e.g. Divorce helpline and mentoring*]			
In whose name?			
First draft received/date:			
Corrections made/date:			
Final copy approved/date:			
Sent to layout house/date:			
Property department			
Article: [*e.g. At last, property market is on the move again or Working with others to ensure a smooth transaction*]			
In whose name?			
First draft received/date:			
Corrections made/date:			
Final copy approved/date:			
Sent to layout house/date:			
Employment department			
Article: [*e.g. Severance packages, compromise agreements and the employee*]			
In whose name?			
First draft received/date:			
Corrections made/date:			
Final copy approved/date:			
Sent to layout house/date:			

	Current issue (date)	Next issue (date)	Following issue (target date)
Commercial department			
Article: [e.g. *Services to business (accountants)*]			
In whose name?			
First draft received/date:			
Corrections made/date:			
Final copy approved/date:			
Sent to layout house/date:			
News about the firm [e.g.: *Have you registered as a client?* *Are you on email?* *Quotable quotes (thank you letters and nice notes, etc.)*]			
First draft received/date:			
Corrections made/date:			
Final copy approved/date:			
Sent to layout house/date:			
First draft received/date:			
Services promotions/service list [*this is what we can do you for*]			
In whose name?			
First draft received/date:			
Corrections made/date:			
Final copy approved/date:			
Sent to layout house/date:			
Good news stories [e.g.: *Mary Stuart qualifies* *A Christmas baby*]			
First draft received/date:			
Corrections made/date:			

	Current issue (date)	Next issue (date)	Following issue (target date)
Final copy approved/date:			
Sent to layout house/date:			
First draft received/date:			

11 How a literature kit can work for your firm

We refer to this promotional material as a 'literature kit' partly to differentiate it from a bound 'firm's brochure' but also to emphasise that it is in fact an integral part of the firm's promotional activity, having bearing as it does on the presentation of the firm and its benefits to past clients, prospects and the PCR, along with the role it has to play in 'cross-selling', underpinning the existing client base and actively seeking recommendation.

11.1 Why a kit and what is it?

Essentially the kit is a folder with a range of loose leaf inserts from which an appropriate selection can be made to make up a personalised presentation or aide memoire for each client, prospect or member of the PCR.

In this way firms can avoid sending irrelevant and even 'damaging' material into the outside world. For example, the professional property developer does not need to know how caring a firm is towards Mrs Jones, a recently bereaved client, and could even be put off by the 'soft/caring' approach. In turn Mrs Jones may be put off by the fear of fees charged by 'commercial solicitors'. They both lose out, but the firm loses most.

Consider how different it might have been if the material sent to each had been more specific and selected more carefully. No one minds that you have differing services and even approaches to different markets. Clients do not mind because, for example, on your website they only select those pages they are interested in. With promotional material provided by firms, clients will read what they are given and too often conclude 'they don't understand my needs at all' and that 'they have simply sent me anything to hand'.

Many things can quickly go out-of-date, through changes in the law to the resignation of a partner, and for a brochure that would mean a full reprint, but with literature kit inserts it just means a tiny adjustment.

11.2 The concept

A literature kit can be, in its best executions, even more than a sales kit.

Effectively there are three types of inserts:

1. Promotional.
2. Information.
3. Procedural.

Only the first is a sales insert in that it deals with benefit presentation (see **Chapter 1**).

Information inserts go that much further and provide additional information that is not required by the casual enquirer but provide a great service through understanding to an actual client.

Procedural inserts are for clients only, explaining the procedures of their matter. All three have an important role to play in the 'client journey', for they enhance client care and are evidence of a firm's proactivity.

11.3 Literature kit usage

There are five main areas where the use of the literature kit can be of real assistance to the firm, and indeed to its clients.

11.3.1 Promotion

A literature kit can be extremely useful in all three tiers of promotion, be it corporate promotion, market-pursued promotion or product-specific promotion (see **Chapter 7**). Indeed the use of a literature kit, as opposed to a brochure, makes this type of targeted promotion possible.

11.3.2 Explanation

When a literature kit is being sent or given to an existing client and the information is related to an existing matter, there is great opportunity for simplifying the explanation about the matter by the production and inclusion of additional inserts. These inserts would include explanations based upon 'things you need to know' and also procedural matters such as things you/we must do.

11.3.3 Cross-selling

The literature kit should help members of a firm understand the benefits of the services offered by departments other than their own. This should aid and increase cross-selling.

The kit itself can help in cross-selling, and assist to avoid the terrible comment 'I didn't know you did that'.

By simply including an insert entitled, 'Services we offer' or 'Departments of the firm' you are providing an aide memoire of the services you have to offer outside the existing matter.

11.3.4 Client contact

The use of a literature kit ensures continual and ongoing client contact. The importance of including a personalised letter within the pack should not be ignored. This can encourage a client to think in terms of using the firm for other matters, and recommending it.

11.3.5 Seeking recommendation

Literature kits should be used in addition to client contact and in conjunction with the PCR. It is intended that these should remind the PCR of the services your firm has to offer, of the benefits they confer and why the members of the PCR should recommend their clients/customers to your firm.

11.4 Training

This is not a brochure and, used best, it is also far more than a series of leaflets. However, this best usage depends in part on the training staff receive on utilising the kits.

Once the kit has been finalised, a full set of inserts in a folder should be provided to each member of staff along with an indication of how and where each insert should be used.

Annex 11A
Literature kit insert checklist

The following list is not exhaustive. It may well be that you require additional or specific inserts that are not listed.

In the same way it is not proposed that any firm should produce all the following inserts as it is unlikely that any firm would require them all.

Introductory inserts

- About the firm
- About the partners
- How to contact us
- About our support staff
- The services we have to offer
- Services for the private client
- The client registration scheme
- Introduction to the welcome pack of client registration scheme
- Divorce helpline

Conveyancing

- Property sales
- Purchases of property
- Leases
- Commercial property
- Residential property
- Buying your home
- Selling your home
- Title defects
- Rights to buy
- Remortgages
- Properties abroad

Probate

- Our services for the older client
- Planning ahead for a more secure future
- Family homes and the elderly
- Caring for the elderly
- Ordering your affairs
- A free affairs assessment
- Management of financial matters

- Probate and the administration of estates
- Making a will
- Lasting powers of attorney
- Settling a person's affairs after death
- Preparation of wills and living wills
- Deeds of gift
- Formation and management of trusts and settlements
- Inheritance tax planning
- Contested probate

Family and social welfare

- Matrimonial and family law
- Family law
- Marriage problems
- Matrimonial and mediation
- Relationship problems and domestic violence
- Divorce
- Divorce helpline
- Matrimonial transfer
- Separation agreements
- Financial settlements
- Maintenance
- Child protection and care
- Court of protection
- Child support agency agreements
- Child care
- Child residency
- Child contact
- Adoption
- Co-habitation

Company and commercial

- The commercial department
- Services to businesses
- Directors' responsibilities
- Company formation
- Business structure and management
- Trade practice and development
- Company taxation
- Terms and conditions of trading

Insolvency

- Insolvency
- Personal and corporate insolvency
- Public guardianship office work (e.g. appointment of receivers)
- Debt collection

Employment

- Employment contracts
- Employment law and the employee
- Employment law and the employer
- Unfair/constructive dismissal claims
- Redundancy
- Discrimination on wage claims
- Compliance and transfer of undertakings
- Protection of employment
- Employment law changes
- Contract review
- Preparing and conducting employment tribunal cases
- Discrimination cases

Mergers and acquisitions

- Sales and purchase of businesses
- Mergers
- Acquisitions
- Management buyouts
- Partnership agreements
- Partnership dissolution
- Partnership and corporate disputes
- Personal injury
- Personal injury compensation
- Motoring cases
- Road traffic accidents
- Motor insurance bureau disputes
- Criminal injuries compensation claims
- Industrial injury and disease
- Tripping accidents
- Private client litigation

Civil litigation

- Contract disputes
- Domestic and commercial property disputes
- Commercial litigation
- Alternative dispute resolution
- Agency and distribution agreements

Others

- Construction law
- Welfare and immigration
- European law

Annex 11B
Literature kit master checklist

> The following checklist may be of assistance in developing a new literature kit, or updating an existing one.

- List of inserts required from each departmental head.
- List of inserts required for each service provided (product).
- List of additional firm-wide inserts.
- Consider which inserts to produce in-house or to have reprinted.
- What printer or systems technology is required to print colour pages in-house?
- Consider what is the best use of the literature kit approach per department.
- Gather wording and research the copy required for each insert with head of each department.
- Use your benefit list to develop a user-friendly literature kit.
- Brief graphic designer/layout artist.
- Brief copywriter if appropriate.
- Get quotes from printers for the folder (which must be printed out-of-house) and the supply of pre-printed inserts (if appropriate).
- Discuss and plan the training for the literature kit with each member of staff.
- Discuss and plan the implementation of literature kit usage by department.
- Establish the monitoring process required to ensure that the kit is used correctly.

12 How a client registration scheme (CRS) can work for your firm

12.1 What is the scheme?

The client registration scheme (CRS) involves the allocation of individually numbered registration cards (usually the size of a credit card) to each individual registered client.

This may be a loyalty or privilege card, but more often it is a simple contact card bearing an inscription similar to 'In the event of my incapacitation or an accident please contact my solicitor [*name of firm*] on [*telephone number*] who holds all my details.' As noted above, the card also carries a client registration number that helps identify that individual.

This provides a genuine and free of charge service which can be extended by a register of the client's 'life's documentation' (see the questionnaire in **Annex 12B**).

This approach ensures that the client keeps the card with your name and telephone number in their wallet or purse at all times. Therefore when a legal need or a request for a recommendation arises, you are close at hand.

The CRS is questionnaire driven (see **Annex 12B**). This questionnaire carries caveats that ensure the client is in control of the completion of the questionnaire and that they do not need to answer any questions they consider inappropriate or impertinent. (In practice most respondents do complete the questionnaire, as people are used to being asked questions by their doctor and solicitor.)

The completed questionnaires, which are of course kept confidential, provide a real insight into clients and their potential needs and this is an important and powerful marketing tool.

At a very minimum the client can be written to, in addition to all the other promotional activity, outlining what information is kept about the client and suggesting that the firm be informed of any updating required.

By offering to keep the actual documentation (wills, deeds, trusts, etc.) or a register of where they are kept, clients receive an additional and genuine benefit while at the same time are further encouraged to think of your firm as 'their solicitor'.

12.2 Why a CRS is needed or should at least be considered

- People like to belong to 'clubs' and feel secure in the knowledge that other people have made the same choice.
- The CRS could be considered a club with various member benefits and, interestingly, people have a habit of being loyal to their clubs.
- It is this 'lost loyalty' from clients towards solicitors that you must seek to replace with the CRS.
- A registered client will always think of your firm as 'their solicitor'.
- The 'new competition' can never achieve this being, as they are, call-centre based, usually miles away from the client.
- The CRS can replace the long gone 'family solicitor syndrome' with a modern, proactive, benefit-based proposal as to why the client should remain with your firm and indeed recommend it to others.
- The CRS, because of the detailed information on a client that it provides, can assist greatly in cross-selling. Potentially it could even define which of your private clients could assist with the placing of commercial work.
- You can continue your campaign of *actively* seeking recommendations in the certain knowledge that a 'card carrying' registered client is far more likely to make that recommendation than someone who vaguely remembers using you a few years ago (and has not heard from you since).
- The CRS provides the perfect opportunity, being questionnaire-based, of turning a tired mailing list into a true database and client relations management (CRM) system.
- By establishing and using a CRS, your firm will ultimately have a significant number of people who will both use you (or considering using you first) and recommend you without hesitation. Why? Because they know, understand and trust you, having found you to be proactive in your client care and handling, in addition to all your other qualities.

Annex 12A
Client registration scheme covering letter

We at [name of firm] are very proud to introduce a scheme which is free of charge to you, and which we believe provides a range of genuine benefits for our clients.

Enclosed you will find a questionnaire. Please note that there is no compulsion to answer all, or even any of the questions. You can become a registered client simply by providing your name and address and telling us that you wish to be registered.

That said, the more we know about our clients, the more we are able to provide them with best advice and we can consider more deeply the areas that are appropriate and important to that client; however, it is up to you.

The benefits to you of the [name of firm] client registration scheme are numerous.

Quick access to your lawyer

Simply quoting your name and registration number will enable us to immediately access your details and those of any matter in hand.

Proactive advice

Because of the information that you have provided us with in your client registration questionnaire we will be able to be proactive on your behalf in the advice we give and the services we offer. We consider our clients as people with a range of needs, rather than a matter in hand to be dealt with as quickly as possible.

In-depth advice

With more detailed knowledge about you, we will be much better placed to advise you fully and promptly when dealing with any matter on your behalf, or considering matters that might arise in the future.

Safe documentation

As a registered client of [name of firm] you will benefit from knowing that all of 'life's documentation' will be listed and held safely in our strong-room. This may include wills, trusts, deeds, life policies, share certificates, living wills, lasting powers of attorney, etc.

Assessment of affairs

Of particular importance is a registered client's entitlement to a free of charge preliminary discussion on any legal matter within a wide range of services provided by [*name of firm*]. This meeting allows you to discuss matters with one of our senior lawyers in the knowledge that you will not be running up a bill, until we have established what legal assistance is needed and that we can supply it to you. At that stage, we will provide an estimate of fees, either on a fixed fee basis or by way of an hourly rate.

A further innovation for the registered client is our free of charge 'affairs assessment'. We believe this to be a great opportunity for our clients to be wide-ranging in the topics they may wish to discuss, and on which we can advise. Briefly, the affairs assessment entitles registered clients to a free meeting, usually with a partner, lasting up to half an hour, by appointment at our offices. At the assessment we will cover all aspects of the legal services we provide, but it is intended to provide the client with the chance to talk freely with an experienced and independent professional.

Free of charge seminars

From time to time we will be holding seminars, the content of which will be of particular interest to certain clients. You will be told in advance of these seminars which will be free of charge to registered clients.

Regular newsletter

The [*name of firm*] newsletter is designed to provide information about current legal situations and changes in the law. It also covers aspects of both the work we undertake, and the people who are here to serve you. Registered clients automatically receive each copy free of charge.

Aftercare service

Increasingly, it has become the practice for firms to charge for the storage and retrieval of clients' files and legal documents, such as wills and property deeds. As a registered client of [*name of firm*] no charge will be made for the retrieval of files from the storage and we will include a free discussion of matters concerned with the file that has been retrieved, should you wish. There is also no charge to registered clients for the storage of property deeds.

Security and assistance

An additional benefit of the registration scheme is security. Important contacts such as your next of kin, doctor, bank manager, accountant, employer, etc. can also be recorded so that in the event of an unforeseen happening we will be able to assist those trying to help you.

A little prompt

Because of the registered information we will keep about you, we are able to 'prompt' during any meeting with you, should we believe action might be required, for example, in making or updating a will, establishing a lasting power of attorney, considerations relating to inheritance tax planning, issues that affect you as an employer, or employee and of course any potential litigious matter.

Registration card

Last, but certainly not least, each registered client is provided with a registration card, similar to a credit card. This, we would suggest, you keep in your purse or wallet at all times. It carries the message 'In the event of an accident or emergency please contact my solicitor quoting my client registration number', along with our telephone number and address. Whatever the circumstances we are here to help you.

Annex 12B
Example client registration scheme questionnaire

Please read this questionnaire carefully, but be assured that there is absolutely no obligation on you to complete all, or any, of the questions. You may wish merely to register as a client and you are most welcome to do so by simply completing your name and address details. We have no wish to be impertinent, and if you would prefer us not to have certain information, please leave the answer to the relevant question blank. All information that you do provide will be held in the strictest confidence and in accordance with the requirements of the Data Protection Act 1998. The information held will be used by us solely to provide you with information and to assist us in advising you on legal issues.

Your details				
Mr/Mrs/Miss/Ms/other (please specify):				
First name(s):				
Surname:				
Address:				
Town:				
County:				
Postcode:				
Home telephone number:				
Home fax:				
Home email:				
Mobile telephone number:				
Date of birth:				
Marital status:	Married ☐		In civil partnership ☐	
	Single ☐		Separated ☐	
	Divorced ☐		Widowed ☐	
Is your spouse/partner a registered client of [name of firm]?	Yes ☐ No ☐			

Your employment details (if applicable)		
If self-employed are you:	Sole trader ☐ In a partnership ☐ Limited company ☐ Other: _____	
Company/business name:		
Address:		
Town:		
County:		
Postcode:		
Job title:		
Telephone number:		
Email address:		
Website address:		
If employed position held:		
Activity of the business:		
Your spouse/partner/next of kin		
Please give details of spouse or partner, if none insert details of your next of kin, i.e. the person you would like us to contact in the event of an accident or emergency.		
Mr/Mrs/Miss/Ms/other (please specify):		
First name(s):		
Surname:		
Relationship:		
Address:		
Town:		
County:		
Postcode:		
Home telephone number:		
Daytime telephone number:		
Mobile telephone number:		
Your dependants		
Number of children:		
First child's full name:		
Date of birth:		

Second child's full name:	
Date of birth:	
If you have more than two children please use other information box and/or separate sheet of paper.	
Do you have any other dependents, e.g. aged parents or relations?	Yes ☐ No ☐
If yes, please answer the relevant questions below.	
Name:	
Relationship to you:	
If you have more than one dependant please use other information box and/or separate sheet of paper.	

Your asset details

Value of main home:	
Outstanding mortgage on main home:	
With whom is your mortgage?	
Do you have a second property?	Yes ☐ No ☐
If yes, please answer the relevant questions below.	
Value of second property	
Outstanding mortgage on second property	
If you have more than two properties please use other information box and/or separate sheet of paper.	
Approximate value of non-property investments held:	
Details of any other assets:	
Please indicate approximate total value:	
Are your assets jointly owned?	Yes ☐ No ☐
If yes with whom?	
If more than one person please give details in the other information box and/or separate sheet of paper.	

Life's documentation

Where are the deeds to your property held?	
National Insurance number:	
Passport number:	
Driving licence number:	

Where are your passport and driving licence kept?	
Where are your birth/marriage certificates and any family death certificates kept?	
Where are your car, life and health insurance documents and their identification numbers kept?	
Where are your share certificates, pension policies and trust documents with their identification numbers kept?	
Do you have a will?	Yes ☐ No ☐
When was it last updated?	
Where is it kept?	
Do you have a living will?	Yes ☐ No ☐
When was it last updated?	
Where is it kept?	
If you have an enduring/lasting power of attorney please fill in the details of your attorney below.	
Mr/Mrs/Miss/Ms/other (please specify):	
Initials:	
Surname:	
Address:	
Town:	
Country:	
Postcode:	
Telephone number:	
If you have more than one attorney please use other information box and/or separate sheet of paper.	
Your advisors' details	
Bank	
Name:	
Town:	
Sort Code:	

Accountant	
Name:	
Town:	
Financial advisor	
Name:	
Town:	
Stockbroker	
Name:	
Town:	
Insurance broker	
Name:	
Town:	
Doctor	
Name:	
Address:	
Town:	
Postcode:	
Should we contact your doctor in the event of an emergency?	Yes ☐ No ☐
Other	
Your planned retirement age:	
Other information:	

Thank you for completing this questionnaire. The information provided will be stored exclusively on the [*name of firm*] database and you will be reminded of it annually. Should you, at any time, wish to alter or remove information you may simply request this and it will be done immediately.

13 Serving the elderly client market

As we all know this is the largest growing demographic group, but what is meant by 'elderly'?

Clearly, there are elderly clients who need numerous services, and often require a dedicated delivery, through such things as home visits. They may have need of services peripheral to 'standard' legal products, such as financial management or other support, and more often than not association with this group culminates in probate.

Then there are those who care for the elderly, such as family members, friends or in a professional capacity, and perhaps make decisions on their behalf.

The term 'middle age' is very unspecific and perception varies greatly with individuals, based, at least in part, on how old they are themselves. This is the planning stage for wills, LPAs, trusts, etc.

Our target therefore in serving this market is fairly broad, taking in as it does immediate users, people planning to use the services and those advising on doing so.

Approaching this market can therefore be seen as a good example of both market-specific promotion and product-specific promotion (see **Chapter 7**). This is also a good example of multi-faceted campaigns.

13.1 Packaging your services

Many services can be required at any age, but looking at the elderly client market would suggest looking at general retirement planning and life beyond retirement covering such things as:

- wills;
- probate;
- inheritance tax planning;
- powers of attorney;
- advanced directives;
- care home provision;
- financial management;
- other support.

By packaging these services together, a firm is demonstrating an understanding of the client's needs and the experience and expertise that the firm has to offer in serving these needs.

They can be packaged together in promotional material, at seminars, in literature and on your website. There can even be a 'virtual', or an actual, department dealing with these matters. This is to demonstrate and offer a 'one stop' solution.

You now have a 'product' to promote.

13.2 Targeting the older market

By using a slogan or by-line such as 'Planning ahead – for a comfortable later life' the full range of services can be incorporated and all sections of the potential market reached.

13.3 The promotional process

Below is a case study of this type of promotion. It is not suggested that every firm will have the resources to undertake the full promotional programme outlined, but it is indicative of what can be done, and is an actual successful campaign run recently.

The firm started by publishing a well-presented booklet entitled 'Planning ahead – for a comfortable later life'.

As you might imagine from the title the subject matter was very much as listed at **13.1** but included additional items on care home fees, equity release schemes, funeral bonds and an important section on why the firm itself was well-positioned to service all the needs of elderly clients through its specialised department. This publication also placed emphasis on starting your planning early and the importance and involvement of carers in the plans. The publication, which was full colour print, incorporated photographs of members of the department and other graphics.

Finally the publication included a freepost tear-off coupon which elicited a surprising number of replies.

Importantly, the firm had put in place a swift and careful response system which was also used for monitoring the success of the campaign.

Initially the firm's well-managed client database was searched for appropriate clients who then received a free copy of the booklet with a covering letter from the fee earner most recently in contact with that client.

'Planning ahead' itself was featured quite heavily in the next edition of the firm's newsletter, which resulted in additional requests for copies from other members of the database.

The newsletter was also sent to the appropriate sections of the firm's PCR, again, with a covering letter but this time with an offer of the provision of a quantity of booklets for distribution around the contact's own client/customer base. Because the booklet was well thought out, well presented and of genuine value to the reader, the take up from the PCR was considerable.

An editorial about the booklet was obtained in the local weekly newspaper and because of the response to that, a series of small and inexpensive advertisements was placed. While the advertising was relatively cheap and probably worth doing, it is important to recognise that in terms of cost per enquiry this route was by far the most expensive. It is, of course, important to note that a record of where enquiries came from was being kept.

The next initiative was a mailing out to all care homes and sheltered accommodation, including a small supply of 'Planning ahead' and including a re-order form which produced an enormous response.

The firm then ran a series of seminars based upon and distributing 'Planning ahead'. The first of these seminars was held for the firm's clients and prospects but the same material was also used in a series of joint seminars with a local and trusted financial advisor. This took 'Planning ahead' to a far wider audience and the seminars were reported on in both the local press and subsequently in a later edition of the firm's own newsletter, enabling the firm to keep alive the message about 'Planning ahead'.

Eventually 'Planning ahead – for a comfortable later life' became so well known that the commercial partner felt able to discuss it with some of his commercial clients. This resulted in two of the commercial clients having special editions of 'Planning ahead' produced for distribution within their own organisations, incorporating their own logos, but heavily promoting the firm concerned.

There was one more vital component to this campaign, and that was that the senior partner was so proud of the booklet that, prior to its launch, he closed the office for lunchtime and invited the entire staff to a light buffet at which he presented the booklet and the campaign to everyone. In fact, he sold the campaign to the staff who all went away with their own copy of 'Planning ahead', enthusiastic about it and their firm's proactive stance. Staff were then kept involved by being informed via email of the outcome, numerically, of each component of the campaign.

Annex 13A
Elderly client market campaign checklist

> **Note:** There are of course many ways of approaching an identified market, such as the elderly client market. This is only one example, but a successful one. The stages and process outlined in this template illustrate one campaign, but can be adapted for use as a checklist for your own individual campaign.

- What services do you provide that could form part of the 'product' you offer to the elderly client market?
- What capacity do you have to increase fee earning from each?
- Is your database able to define appropriate clients?
- If not, do you have a mailing list?
- Who will coordinate this campaign?
- Should you form a 'virtual' department?
- Who will head that?
- Does your PCR include care homes and sheltered accommodation?
- What distribution methods will you use?
- How can this campaign be extended?
- Should you consider a campaign to the care homes and sheltered accommodation you are in contact with?
- How can these contacts be extended?
- Who can/will present the seminar?
- Have all fee earners in the department been informed of this promotional initiative?
- Have they been trained in their role relating to it?
- Who is responsible for the production of your equivalent to 'Planning ahead'?
- Will it be distributed instead of or in addition to your regular newsletter?
- When will it be distributed to the PCR and who will write the covering letter?
- Are press releases for the local press ready along with a list of named editors?
- How will you monitor this campaign?

14 Advertising, sponsorship, press and public relations

There are two important points to remember before even considering your promotional activity. Both have been referred to already in the toolkit, but in different contexts. They are vital and therefore worth repeating.

First, the purpose of the activity, whichever media is decided upon, is to express and present benefits along with an appropriate 'call to action'. There is no other point to promotion. Even those dreadful concepts of 'waving the flag' or 'raising profile' demand benefit presentation and your promotional activity should be more focused than that anyway.

The second lesson learned earlier in this toolkit is that your services are a derived need (see **Chapter 1**) and that generally speaking you cannot influence that need, or increase the demand for your services. Therefore you have to seek to speak to those who have already decided on a course of action that demands legal work and persuade them, through the presentation of sufficient and appropriate benefits, that you are the supplier they should choose from the vast range of alternatives.

Relating these facts to the purchase of advertising space, in for example a local newspaper, provides a salutary, budgetary, lesson. Perhaps the readership of the newspaper is 150,000 and that is substantial. How many of those have decided to move house/get a divorce/make a will, etc. and therefore need a solicitor at this time (during the life of that issue)? Estimating 10 per cent of that readership would seem to be generous. Of the average 50 pages in a local paper, how many are read in any detail, by what percentage of the total readership? Research suggests that between 10 and 50 per cent of the content is not seen at all by at least 50 per cent of the readership and that retention of any given message is again relatively low. It would therefore seem that the chances of contacting anyone with a specific need for your services at this time are very slim. Of course, for suppliers of high volume items these readership figures are perfectly acceptable but for those providing a derived need they are not, in that they are far too 'scattershot'. The odds need to be increased by far greater targeting. Of course, you may feel that featuring in every issue in a fixed spot rather than 'run of paper', will provide an additional 'directory' advertisement, so that people will know where to look when, at last, they do have a 'derived' need for your services. A valid point, but you will need a big budget.

There are many different types of public promotion including, of course, advertising, which is usually defined as paid-for space in the media, i.e. newspapers and magazines, including trade or professional press, together with directories (Yellow Pages, Thomson Local, the phone book, etc.), radio, local and national TV and the internet (e.g. Google AdWords), plus anywhere else where you can pay for space and define the content of your message, e.g. billboards, buses, blotters, beer mats (and that is just the 'Bs').

In fairness, blotters and beer mats would probably be considered as promotion, despite carrying advertising, and rate alongside your literature kit, website and newsletter. Other forms of promotion include seminars, exhibitions, open days and, if not a junket, then client and professional contact entertaining.

'Press relations' makes use of all the media listed above under advertising, but seeks unpaid coverage through news releases. The words 'news release' are worth remembering. They are often referred to as 'press releases', but they are unlikely to get published if they are simply advertisements slightly disguised. They must contain news and be newsworthy to stand even a chance of publication.

There is one grey area which applies mostly to local media and trade press, which may be your main target. This is what is sometimes referred to as 'advertorial', i.e. paid-for space that is presented as a feature or editorial coverage linked to an advertisement in a different part of the publication.

But of all methods of public promotion, the most important is personal selling. Indeed, it could be argued that every other form of promotion is geared primarily to getting a face-to-face meeting with a client prospect or professional contact.

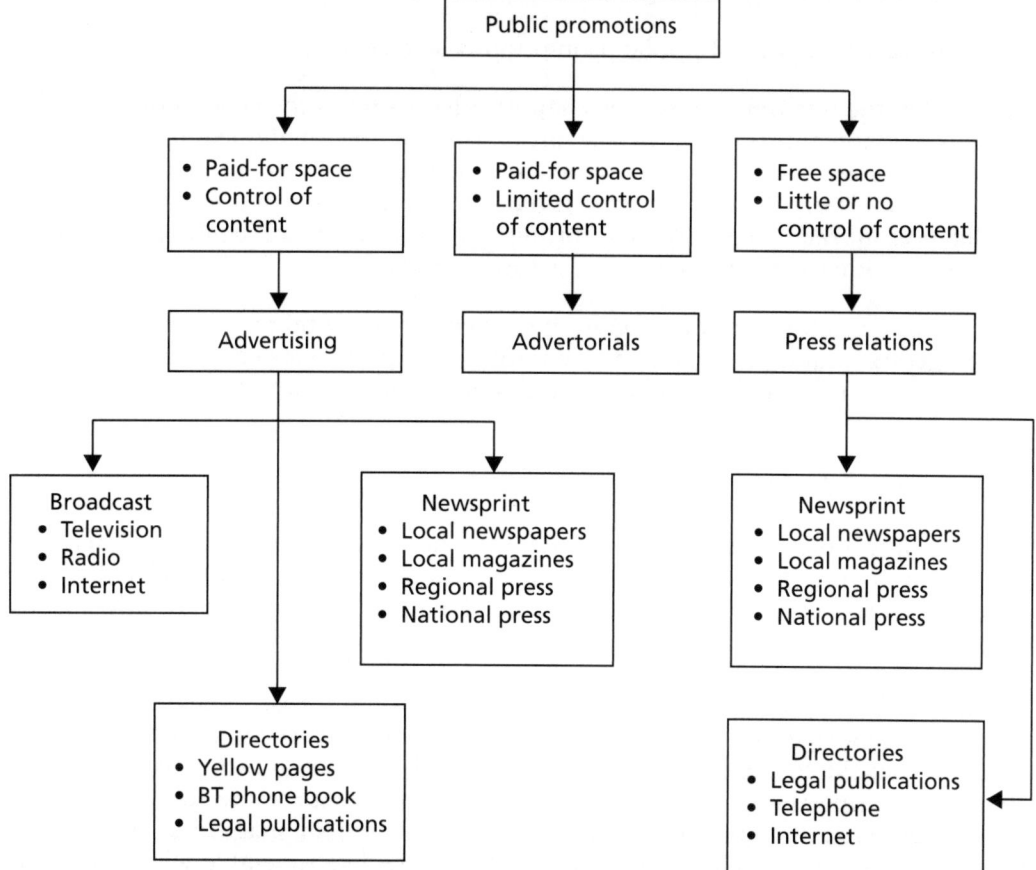

Figure 14.1: Hierachy of promotional methods

Figure 14.1 illustrates and explains the most commonly used forms of public promotion and the media associated with it. There are some items that are not included. For example, while business gifts are a promotional item they more properly belong alongside your website, literature kit and newsletter in that they are not truly 'public'. In the same way that billboards and buses are advertising, they are specialist and unlikely to be used by most practices.

So for the purpose of considering the planning of public promotion we will confine ourselves to the following:

- *Advertising:* paid-for space with control over content.
- *Advertorials:* paid-for (or part paid-for space) with limited control (usually involving the publications editor) over content.
- *Public relations:* free, but little or no control over content.

To this list, although not on the chart, we need to add sponsorship, which can be used in conjunction with such things as 'client away days' or even seminars.

14.1 Advertising

The most obvious form of public promotion is advertising.

As noted in the introduction to this chapter, advertising in the general or corporate sense is seldom appropriate for the promotion of the small/medium sized legal practice. Despite this it can be beneficial when it is used to promote a specific product to a clearly defined target market. The presentation of a 'divorce helpline' or defence in the licence points totting up procedure are examples. General advertising, other than in directories, is too scattershot.

The exception to this is a special edition or special feature that will in itself produce the targeting required, although even this should be viewed with scepticism, especially when the space is being offered at a discount on a very tight deadline.

14.1.1 The 'blackmail budget'

There is one other area of advertising that needs consideration, unflatteringly referred to as the 'blackmail budget' in this toolkit, which is also related to the purchase of space usually in printed media. Frequently the request to advertise is received from a friend, a client or a professional contact. The space is then purchased, not because there is any real or measurable chance of gaining meaningful additional business, but because to say 'no' would cause embarrassment or potentially damage the relationship with an important client or contact. It is assumed that the firm will gain no new business, but it can in fact enhance a firm's chances by using the space in the 'blackmail budget' to promote solely the firm's website address. Perhaps then the readers of the parish magazine, the theatre programme, the rugby club fixture list or the village fete timetable will notice and remember the firm.

More positively, it must be recognised that the one certain benefit all advertising has, providing it is of good quality, is the underpinning of your existing client base. The truth is that people who already use you are most likely to note your advertisement and seeing the benefits clearly demonstrated will assist readers in believing that they have made the right decision and therefore increase their feelings of goodwill towards you.

14.1.2 Newspapers

There is of course a vast range of newspapers (and other publications) which can be investigated at **www.brad.co.uk**

National newspapers, generally speaking, are unlikely to be of interest to 'high street' solicitors, except perhaps as part of a national campaign.

Regional editions of national papers provide a less expensive way of appearing in your own area in what is, to all intents and purposes, a national paper.

More likely, however, will be the utilisation of the local press and here the mix is likely to be a variety of product-specific advertising and general advertorials.

Additionally, there are hand-delivered 'freebies', which to be frank, historically have a very downmarket reputation. Then there are of course national magazines, regional versions of them and, perhaps of particular interest for product-specific advertising such as a 'divorce helpline', the regional or county press. (Colour county magazines have produced some surprisingly good results in the promotion of divorce-related matters.) Finally, there are trade or special interest newspapers and magazines but the likelihood of a firm needing to advertise to a firm's own profession, other than for recruitment, seems extremely unlikely.

14.1.3 Directories

This is a form of advertising that may still be of considerable value to an individual legal practice. Not long ago when discussing directories we would be talking about the printed versions of Yellow Pages and Thomson Local, etc. However, the importance and focus has now of course moved to the internet. Inclusion in printed directories continues to be essential to those people already committed to considering your firm, and therefore requiring a telephone number, but of even more importance is entry in the internet listings categories, ideally with links to your own website.

14.1.4 Billboards, posters and advertising on the buses

If your existing brand image is strong enough within your own geographical area, these forms of advertising, provided they are product-based, can be effective. They are likely to need to be part of a campaign that is featured in other media at the same time, and must be clearly understood with a specific easy 'call to action' such as 'Fixed price conveyancing, ring for free half hour interview', or 'Need advice on a divorce? Ring us free now' and of course 'No win – No fee'.

The obvious problem is all this has a very downmarket feel, and it is important that one department of the firm does not damage the image of the rest of the practice through its own 'pile 'em high, sell 'em cheap' approach. Generally speaking these appear to be inappropriate media for the majority of firms.

14.1.5 Radio and television

Local radio and television are very accessible. There is no reason why a promotional message should not be presented through the media but it does need very careful monitoring and strict budgetary controls. Again it cannot be generic or general, and must be product-specific.

14.1.6 Advertorials

Advertorials, or 'aditorials', are either advertisements in paid-for space but set to look like articles, or articles written about the firm or the subject it is advertising linked to an advertisement. This practice is covered by specific legislation, rules and codes of practice. For example, an advertisement set to look like an article must have the words 'advertisement feature' set above it.

However, despite this, they can be useful because when mixed with specific product advertising they can 'occasionally' provide more detail, insight, and perhaps actual (non-named) case histories.

14.2 Public relations

Public relations (PR) covers a wide range of specialist disciplines including media relations, customer communications, investor relations, government lobbying, staff communications and even the unnervingly titled 'crisis PR'. Probably the most relevant aspect of PR for the high street practice is media and press relations. Unlike advertising, this is an attempt to get unpaid, 'independent', editorial coverage in the local media. Properly done, it is a potentially valuable tool in the marketing mix, but the ground rules of dealing with journalists need to be understood. Moreover, unlike advertising or advertorials where the message is fully controlled by the advertiser, there is no certainty that your press release will be used at all or, if it is used, that the final story comes out the way you hoped it would.

To avoid the pitfalls and disappointments it is worth having some insight into how an editor or journalist works. First, you must appreciate that the typical local paper or magazine is deluged with hundreds of press releases a week. The main problem for journalists is to filter through the junk, spam and general corporate advertising 'puff' to get to something that is worth their circulation reading.

That said, if you get media relations right, it could provide you with fantastic 'free' coverage that boosts your firm's profile, helps existing and potential clients understand what you do and gives staff a boost. Remember, most people buy newspapers and magazines to read the news not to look at advertisements, so a story about your practice is more likely to be noticed than an expensive advertisement. It is also more likely to be believed as more credibility is given to an impartial editorial.

Not only do relevant press releases create positive awareness, but they also stimulate invitations to provide information for other articles. By building confidence with the individual editors and journalists, you may also be asked to comment on other stories that do not start from you. Your senior partner or head of department can become a reliable 'pundit' on topical affairs or local happenings once credibility has been established. Establishing it is, of course, a long-term project.

It is worth learning a few basics about writing successful press releases. Journalism is more an art than a science and it may well be that you wish to employ a specialist. However, while there are some naturally more gifted writers than others, an effective press release can be written by most intelligent laymen with a little thought and practice.

So, whether you are writing the release yourself or approving matter written by someone else you have briefed, put yourself in the busy editor's seat, wading through piles of releases that are received every day.

There are certain key criteria the editor is looking for:

- Relevance.
- Timeliness.
- Readability.
- Presentation.

Relevance to the publication and topicality are essential. The editor is thinking 'Are my readers interested in this?'

For your press releases to be successful, you must learn to grab the attention of the editor or journalist and ultimately that of the reader, quickly. Well-written stories that are genuine news stories and press releases start by providing the essence of the story in a nut shell. The enduring press release mantra runs:

- Who?
- What?
- When?
- Where?
- Why?
- How?

The headline and first paragraph should answer all those questions, or as many of them as possible. After this immediate summary of the story, use the next three or four paragraphs to expand upon events and use one of those to include a quote from a relevant partner or other spokesman. This is an opportunity to convey the firm's wider wisdom and ambition.

Within four or five paragraphs you should be able to tell the full story. Keep the tone neutral and do not resort to corporate 'sales babble' – a press release is not an advertisement.

End the piece clearly by saying where and from whom the journalist can get further information. Always date your press releases.

Traditionally releases are typed with 1.5 or double line spacing to allow the journalist to insert, edit and modify although this is becoming less common with the use of email and word documents.

If you use email, which is very acceptable, do not use complex formatting. Clarity is key and the journalist wants to be able to cut and paste easily. There is no need to send an email with a separate email attachment, though an attached jpeg is acceptable as journalists do like relevant photographs. Finally, make sure you send it to the right person (worth checking beforehand) and do not be afraid of following up with a courteous call. Despite their reputation, most journalists (particularly local ones) do not eat solicitors for breakfast.

14.3 Sponsorship

Sponsorship and events can be a form of public promotion, especially if they are linked to such things as advertising, PR and newsletter articles. They can be very valuable as they are directed at a chosen section of the public, be that geographical, a certain demographic or by interest, and as this is pre-determined, you can ensure that the literature you provide (from your literature kit) is appropriate.

Sponsorship and events are therefore worthy of serious consideration because they can be used to promote your brand in your area, establishing your firm as a local and caring organisation in the face of the national, faceless 'new competition'.

There are many forms of sponsorship from rally cars and racehorses through to hot air balloons, to the sponsorship of a specific animal at Marwell Zoo or a tree in the Sheffield Botanical Gardens. The successful ones have a local connotation and a link which must be demonstrated if it is not obvious to the firm or the department. Supporting the senior partner racing his Aston Martin or his wife's equestrian efforts, while understandable, should not really be part of the promotional budget.

Annex 14A
External promotions audit

> **Note:** The questions in this example promotions audit are very general. Please adapt them to suit you firm.

1. What image does the firm present to its clients?
2. What image would you like to present?
3. How does the firm currently promote itself and its products? (List these in order of importance with, where possible, costs and results.)
4. What is the composition of the current promotional mix?*
5. What marketing budget has been allocated for the current financial year? What proportion of this is for promotional activity?
6. How has the firm traditionally promoted its products to existing clients? (This list will be similar to the one above but allows for each activity and sub-part of each activity to be rated good/average/poor or some similar grading.)
7. How has the firm traditionally promoted its products to new clients?
8. For each product that the firm is currently offering, or intends to offer, what is the relative importance of each element of the promotional mix (advertising, publicity, sales promotion, personal selling)?
9. Does/should the firm advertise?
10. If it should, what should it advertise?
11. How should it advertise?
12. Which media should be used?
13. Should cooperation be considered with other legal firms for the purposes of advertising? (e.g. 'accident lawyers for you', etc.)?
14. Should cooperation be considered with a non-legal firm for the purposes of advertising (care home fees insurance for example)?
15. How much, if anything, should be spent on paid advertising space?
16. How important is personal selling in the firm's chosen market/segments?
17. Who are the people most capable of personal selling (e.g. who are the 'finders, minders and grinders')?
18. What steps should be taken to support and reward your sales force?
19. What steps should be taken to improve the performance of other people currently not considered in the sales role?
20. What steps should be taken to improve the overall capability in the field of personal selling?
21. How important is publicity for the corporate image (brand)?
22. How important is publicity to the individual products?
23. What is the real cost of publicity likely to be?

---

* Generally speaking a promotional mix is made up of advertising, publicity, sales promotion and personal selling. It needs to be related to the corporate image, the department and the market segment. Wherever possible it needs to be quantified and costs/success apportioned.

24. What, if any, sales promotional activity should be evaluated/pursued?
25. What product/markets would benefit from investment in sales or promotional activity?
26. How can the degree of client loyalty be improved (e.g. client registration scheme)?
27. How can you sell more products to existing clients (e.g. newsletters, seminars, cross-selling, etc.)?
28. How can you reach new clients and prospects (e.g. actively seeking recommendation, or the professional contacts register (PCR))?
29. How can you best grow/develop/use your PCR?
30. How can you measure the results of time and money invested in promotion?

15 The personal touch: personal selling and networking

Nobody came into the legal profession to be a salesman. There are still some who view selling and those who perform it with suspicion, feeling perhaps that it has no place in a profession. This attitude would seem to stem from the 'caricature' of the hard-bitten, door-to-door salesman, lying his way to a sale. In reality nothing could be further from the truth.

The truth is, if selling is properly defined, we all 'sell' most of the time. A true definition would be 'the presentation of enough benefits to persuade another to your point of view'. Every parent has seen a five-year old do that.

Selling is a planned and controlled conversation based on the objective of ensuring that your listener has sufficient information to make an informed decision. Arguably, if you have an excellent legal practice and fail to inform people of this fact, thus allowing them to fall into the hands of the less competent, you are being, in its broadest sense, negligent.

Selling is also about listening and gathering the facts so that you can represent the relevant benefits and serve the needs of the prospective client best. There is an old adage from the work of selling: 'you have two ears and one mouth, use them in that proportion'.

Everything in this toolkit so far has been written to assist you in telling people about all you have to offer. But every promotional action you take must end in a conversation of one kind or another. Of course, it is a fact that some people are better than others at dealing with strangers, and some would find public speaking impossible.

As a start to building your 'sales force', it is worthwhile to refer back to the skills and interests audit recommended in **Chapter 3** and included in **Annex 3B**. Remember everyone, including partners, fee earners and support staff, has the potential to influence how the firm is viewed by the outside world.

The purpose of a skills and interests audit is to list the type of activities that everyone involved in the firm has. There is often an opportunity to make a presentation to a club that a fee earner or member of staff belongs to.

Also from this, information relating to sales ability and attitude can be obtained. For example, people involved with amateur dramatics or other theatrical activity are likely to be the type of people who can make a presentation and are unafraid to do so.

The form deliberately avoids a question relating to 'sales ability' as indication of this varies from person to person and analysis of the form is likely to provide answers to that question anyway. Sometimes these answers can be quite surprising: the modest and quietly spoken person may be hopeless on a public platform but perfect in a face-to-face conversation.

At first the noting of home address and postcode may seem irrelevant as this information will undoubtedly be already held by HR. However it does provide an interesting spread of geographical coverage and it is worth noting that someone living in the north of an area is unlikely to be involved in activities, or have the desire to be involved in activities, in the south.

Seeking information about spouses and children may seem 'impertinent', however it is important as a spouse's interest is just as relevant to a firm's current activity as a member of staff's. Also those without children are unlikely to be involved in children activities or parent/teacher associations.

Although it does need to be handled delicately, the interests, activities and memberships of staff members and their spouses can lead to genuine and useful contacts within the community that the firm is seeking to serve. For example, trade associations can often be turned into professional contacts.

Answers to questions relating to favourite clients and type of prospects are illustrative of attitude, and personal strengths and ambitions are both important to note, and are a further indication of the type of person being dealt with. The intention of the audit is not to find the 'wrong type'. Indeed it could be argued that there are no wrong types, from this point of view. It merely seeks, to use an awful American phrase, to define a firm's 'finders, minders and grinders'.

15.1 Preparing a sales presentation

There are of course, many types of sales presentations made in many different situations. These may vary from a quick reference to another service provided by the firm during an existing client meeting, to a full-blown presentation of services that could be provided for a major manufacturer or local institution. The former will obviously be an informal presentation, the latter may see you in a highly competitive situation as part of a 'beauty parade'.

In every case, as with so much else in life, preparation is the key.

15.1.1 Know your product

Everyone will claim that they do, but for the purpose of a sales presentation it is vital to remember that we are not only talking about procedural matters, although they may need to be presented and referred to, but also the product must be presented in terms of the benefits to be derived by the client (see **Chapter 1**).

15.1.2 Know your prospect

Assuming the presentation is with a prospect, the need to research them prior to your meeting is vital. You need to understand the prospect almost as well as you understand a client with whom you are currently working.

Learn about the problems facing that company or its industry and how to demonstrate that understanding.

Be clear about what they are seeking from the meeting and ensure that you more than fulfil those aspirations.

15.1.3 Prepare your actual presentation

Do not leave what you are going to say, or the order you are going to say it, to chance. Think through what you need to convey and practice it.

It is always a good idea to have a sales presenter. Essentially this is a visual aid that will focus all members of the meeting on the subject at hand. It will probably be based upon inserts from your literature kit although it may also include:

- recent successes and developments in the firm;
- an indication of an understanding/experience in the prospect's industry, etc.;
- some referrals from other satisfied clients (with their permission);
- a draft contract;
- a programme of follow-up.

15.1.4 Plan your opening remarks

Once the introductions and courtesies are over you need to take control of the meeting as quickly as possible with a few clear opening remarks, possibly ending with what you want the meeting to cover and achieve. (This can then be referred back to at the end of the meeting.)

15.1.5 Think through likely objections

Objections may be genuine, or simply raised to elicit information about the matters being discussed. If you are experienced in your subject matter then it is unlikely that any brand new objections will be raised, therefore you will be well-placed to carefully consider your answers to objections. It is important however not to appear glib and to ensure that you give the objection, however many times you have heard it before, due consideration and a careful, personalised response as if it was indeed the first time such a thought had ever been raised.

In some circumstances an objection may take the form of a price query or resistance. You should think it through carefully and pre-prepare a presentation of all aspects of the cost justification while remembering that the benefits offered outweigh the price being charged in the mind of the client and instruction should follow.

15.1.6 Target the result of the meeting

Obviously the results of any meeting will depend on the type of meeting that it is. The targeted result for an informal chat with an existing client may be a meeting with a colleague in a different department. At a pre-planned major meeting, the objectives and the likely outcome of the meeting should be very clear, even from the early stage of preparation.

The objective or target of the meeting may not necessarily be an instruction. At an initial meeting you may simply be seeking permission to present a proposal and your presentation in this case will be geared to explaining one way the potential client should agree to a proposal being produced and the benefits that will be gained from that proposal. If it is a contract for the provision of services, then a draft contract should be included in your sales presenter.

15.1.7 Agree next action/plan your follow-up

Your preparation for this meeting should go as far as preparing your next action and your follow-up to that meeting. Agreement to this by both parties will provide a very satisfactory conclusion to the sales presentation, provided the target results of that meeting have been achieved.

15.2 Presenting benefits

This toolkit has emphasised the importance of analysing and understanding benefits. The presentation of these benefits is therefore also extremely important.

There are many occasions when a firm's dealings with clients or prospects will call for the firm to make recommendations, present proposals, or suggest a course of action. The objective is to persuade the client/prospect to take a positive view of the firm's proposals and therefore accept the advice or even, if it is an initial contact, to decide to instruct your firm.

The truth is that the process is very simple. First, establish the needs of your client, and create a desire in the client to satisfy these needs, and then put forward the relevant advantages or benefits of your service which will, demonstrably, satisfy them.

The technique has three steps:

1. State your idea, proposal or advantage.
2. Emphasise the meaning or significance of your proposal in terms of the advantage it will give the client.
3. Ask a question to make sure that the client understands and accepts the advantage or benefit.

This process applies throughout a lot of a firm's dealings with other people, and not just in the area of sales presentation. However as this is the area that we are dealing with here let us adopt this approach and use a sales scenario as an example.

In this case the process can be remembered by the simple mnemonic 'BMQ'.

- State the *benefit*.
- Explain the *meaning* (or significance of the benefit).
- Ask a *question* at the end to gain commitment.

Benefit, Meaning, Question equals the BMQ.

For example:

- *Benefit*: 'Your instructions will only be handled by legally qualified experienced people'.
- *Meaning*: 'This means that you can be secure in the knowledge that the whole job can be handled professionally and comprehensively'.
- *Question*: 'With a purchase as important as a house, we feel that this is far better than entrusting the process to one of these new computerised services – wouldn't you agree?'

15.3 Objections/cost justification

A format similar to the BMQ technique can be used in overcoming objections. As noted at **15.1.5**, objections are quite often voiced in price concerns but can be a sign that the client is interested but requires reassurance of the benefits the firm or service offers.

For example, 'Why are you more expensive than other solicitors?' is possibly the most commonly raised objection. It is likely to occur before the transaction when the prospective client is making a choice between your firm, one of the 'new competition', or even potentially a do-it-yourself approach to law.

The important thing to remember is that this is in fact an invitation to present or represent benefits in the form of cost justification. Here the BMQ technique is developed slightly with the addition of 'yes but'. For example, 'Yes I can see that it may seem expensive but' or 'We should perhaps look together at what you're getting for your money and the dangers of not having the work done properly'.

Done properly this part of this process is an opportunity for a reappraisal of the benefits – it is an opportunity to reassess the client's requirements and for your firm's benefits to be presented again to match those requirements.

As noted at **15.1.3** with the development of a sales presenter, it is very well worth taking the time to do some rehearsal. Be confident in the presentation of your presenter and practice the BMQ and the 'yes but' techniques.

15.4 Networking

There are numerous opportunities for different levels of networking of which you are undoubtedly aware within your own geographical market. These vary from small local 'breakfast clubs' through to national exhibitions, with hundreds of opportunities in between. In fact networking has been the staple business-getter of the legal profession for a long time. Attendees, however, seem to be polarised between those who 'feel they should turn up' and are lucky to get any work as a result and those who pre-prepare carefully and consider networking as one of their prime marketing activities and sources of new business.

The key obviously is preparation. If you know who is going to be attending the event, target those you particularly want to see and prepare a presentation to the correct level of formality, as without a doubt the direct approach is the best one. Everyone is at these networking events to gain something for themselves. As always your job is to demonstrate that you have benefits to offer. Once you have established this you will be listened to.

As with all presentations (even those that come unexpectedly – and they do at networking events) the next and most important part is the follow-up. Conclude your meeting/presentation at the event with the agreement that you will write to the prospect in more detail when you return to your office. It is extremely unlikely that this offer will be refused. Your follow-up should reiterate what you have talked about and the agreements made and ideally include a proposal or an agreement to meet later on a defined date to discuss one.

If a meeting does not conclude that positively, agree that you will write to them periodically (again this is unlikely to be refused). Send them a copy of the appropriate inserts of your literature kit and follow that up with a personalised letter enclosing the latest newsletter and pointing out an article of relevance to them, and write a personal actual letter to them suggesting another meeting. The above three stages should take approximately six months.

Finally keep a 'sales record card' in written or electronic format. This is well worth developing as a habit. Keep all the details of each contact, outline each discussion you have had, record the action agreed to and when it was executed and the follow-up date. Put this into a bring-forward system and you will see your prospect list grow as never before.

Or, you could simply go home and put your feet up! The good news is that many of your traditional competitors do just that.

Annex 15A
Staff attitude audit

Most staff members in any organisation like to believe that they have a full understanding of that organisation and their position in it. Regrettably this is untrue within a large number of organisations, especially within the legal profession where the 'them and us' attitude still seems to exist between partners and staff.

The more you know about your staff and the better your communications with them, the easier it is to improve performance by the correct deployment of assets, skills and attitude.

Clearly this list is only intended to be indicative but it is a start. Staff like to be included and this can be particularly significant such as strategic and promotional planning.

When preparing a sales or other promotional campaign, the partner in charge needs to carefully consider the following:

- What do staff say to clients?
- What do staff say socially about the firm?
- Do the staff share the partisanship vision?
- Do they understand their role in this vision?
- How are they rewarded (this is not just a question of money)?
- Are they the first of the last to know about new promotional campaigns?

Annex 15B
Sales presentation checklist

- Do you really know your 'product' in terms of benefits derived by the client?
- Have you studied the literature kit inserts relating to your presentation and have you made up a kit of inserts in the firm's folder specifically?
- Do you understand the individual or company you are about to visit?
- Do you know the evolution of your firm's relationship with this client/prospect?
- Do you know what work has been undertaken for them in the past?
- Do you know of any great successes you have experienced together?
- Do you know of any failures or problems that have occurred?
- Have you prepared your presentation adequately?
- Have you clearly planned your opening remarks?
- Have you thought through the likely objections and your answers to them?
- Can you produce examples and evidence to back up your assertions?
- What is the targeted result of this meeting?
- What other/ancillary services that your firm offers should you introduce at this meeting?

Annex 15C

Networking checklist

Prior to attending an event that may lead to networking, it is worth considering the following:

- Do you know who you are likely to meet at this event?
- Do you know in general terms the type of person you are likely to meet at this event?
- What is the purpose of you attending this event?
- What is the objective you have (meeting with specific person, etc.)?
- What is the objective of these specific meetings?
- Are you prepared in terms of literature kit, presenter and aide memoire for these meetings?
- Have you prepared your benefits statements related to the features of the services you are offering or your firm in general?
- Do you have a simple method of following up contacts made at networking events?
- Have you prepared yourself to recall the meetings you have at this event?
- Do you have a standardised follow-up system?
- Are there likely to be opportunities to link existing clients/contacts with new contacts made at that networking event?
- Should you study more about the art of sales and presentation benefits?

APPENDIX A

Law Society accreditation schemes: how they can help you to market your practice

Accreditation schemes overview

Part of the marketing plan for your new business should include careful consideration of whether membership to any of the Law Society's accreditation schemes would benefit your business, or is required to obtain Legal Services Commission funding or to work in certain areas of law.

In this section, we shall explore what options are available to you and why you should consider becoming a member.

The Law Society runs two types of accreditation schemes, for individual practitioners and for practices.

Individual-based accreditation schemes

As well as numerous membership networks (otherwise known as Sections) available at the Law Society, there are many voluntary accreditation schemes that individual practitioners and practices can apply to become a member of.

Accreditation schemes for individual practitioners include Children Law, Criminal Litigation, Clinical Negligence, Family Law, Mental Health, Personal Injury, Mediation and many others. By accrediting as an individual practitioner you earn special recognition for your expertise in a specific area of law.

The Law Society operates these individual-based accreditation schemes in order to:

- promote high standards in legal service provision;
- ensure that consumers are easily able to identify legal practitioners with proven competency in given areas of law;
- help consumers to make informed choices;
- offer solicitors and firms use of a recognisable brand;
- provide information for courts, statutory bodies and other professionals;
- ensure that scheme members maintain relevant standards of competency and expertise, by means of periodic reselection and re-accreditation.

Entity-based accreditation schemes

When setting up your legal practice you should consider whether membership of these schemes, and the benefits they bring, would benefit your practice as a business.

The Law Society currently runs two entity-based schemes – the Conveyancing Quality Scheme (CQS) and Lexcel. The Law Society is also looking to launch the Wills and Inheritance Accreditation Scheme (WIAS) in the latter part of 2013/early 2014. We explore the Conveyancing Quality Scheme and Lexcel below.

Conveyancing Quality Scheme

The Conveyancing Quality Scheme (CQS) was launched in late 2010 and its purpose is to provide a recognised quality standard for residential conveyancing practices. Achievement of membership establishes a level of credibility for member practices with stakeholders (regulators, lenders, insurers and consumers) based upon three key areas:

1. The integrity of the Senior Responsible Officer and other key conveyancing staff. The Senior Responsible Officer being an individual at the practice accountable to the Law Society for membership to the scheme.
2. The practice's adherence to good Core Practice Management Standards.
3. Adherence to prudent and efficient conveyancing procedures through the Law Society Conveyancing Protocol.

CQS has created a trusted community of conveyancers which deters fraud and will drive up standards in conveyancing year on year. Each year the Law Society assesses and audits a proportion of its members to ensure adherence to the rigorous standards of the scheme.

The benefits of being a member

There are many benefits to being a member of the CQS. You will become a member of a trusted community of conveyancers that stakeholders such as lenders have confidence in. The Law Society has also seen that having CQS accreditation has increased members' marketing ability to the public which has resulted in an increased client intake. Other benefits include:

- use of CQS branding on letterheads and websites;
- entry on to the Law Society website with a search tool for members of the public;
- quarterly CQS e-newsletter, including news and features;
- CQS events and CPD courses;
- exclusive professional indemnity insurance (PII) product offering;
- qualification for some lenders panels;
- a dedicated CQS Technical helpline.

Further benefits being developed include making online technical solutions such as smart forms available to CQS firms and their clients; further promotion of the scheme to the public; affinity products and solutions; and CQS materials for members to give to clients.

Becoming a member – requirements and process

In order to make an application to the scheme, the applicant practice must be regulated by the Solicitors Regulation Authority.

The practice also has to undertake residential conveyancing work and nominate a Senior Responsible Officer (SRO) and Head of Conveyancing (HOC) for the purposes of the scheme.

Application to the scheme is made by way of application form. The application form can be found on the Law Society's website (**www.lawsociety.org.uk**) and is split into two main elements. The first part relates to provenance and the second to excellence.

In relation to provenance, the applicant is asked to provide information as to the details of the practice's constitution, number of managers, financial information relating to residential conveyancing for the previous three years, information as to referral fees, complaints and PII claims history, amongst other pieces of information.

In relation to excellence, the applicant is also asked to confirm whether it has various policies and procedures under four Core Practice Management Standards. These are financial management, supervision and operation risk management, client care and file and case management.

Together with the application, the applicant needs to submit to the CQS office the practice's PII policy schedule and claims summaries for the previous five years, accounts reports where they are qualified, details as to complaints and CPD records for relevant persons. Further, the applicant firm needs to include in its application details of all relevant people for the purposes of the application. These are all those that are managers/partners at the firm, qualified conveyancers (such as solicitors, CILEx or licensed conveyancers), non-qualified conveyancers, key support staff and accounts staff.

At the time the application is submitted, the SRO needs to either have completed Basic Disclosure checks (Criminal Records Bureau checks) or have instigated obtaining them, for him or herself, the Head of Conveyancing, managers and qualified conveyancers. Results as to those checks will need to be provided to the CQS team before the application can proceed.

Once all information has been provided, the CQS team will consider the application, information provided and conduct further checks. For example, identity checks are carried out on the SRO, HOC and managers. Further a credit check is carried out on the practice and a bank reference obtained should the score be below an accepted level. Additional checks include the inspection of SRA records (in relation to practising certificates and any conditions, complaints and regulatory investigations), checking records with CILEx and the Council of Licensed Conveyancers as appropriate, considering CPD records and further analysis is conducted in relation to PII claims, complaints, regulatory investigations and so on.

Once all information has been considered, a decision is taken to accredit, defer (for up to 12 months) or reject a practice's application for membership. If the application is deferred or rejected, the CQS office will set out the reasons why the practice has not met the required standard and any corrective action that is to be taken.

Upon becoming a member, the Practice Agreement signed by the applicant at the outset comes into force. This Agreement sets out the obligations upon the practice during membership and includes (amongst other things) that the practice agree to update the CQS office every six months in respect of complaints, adhere to the Conveyancing Protocol and that all relevant members of staff will undertake mandatory training. This training is set by the CQS office.

Applying as a new practice

As a new practice, providing some of the information described above will be difficult as it will not have yet occurred. For example, three years' figures for the number of residential conveyancing transactions, five years' PII claims history, complaints history and so on.

Being a newly formed practice is not a bar to being a member of the CQS. However full information must still be provided.

If the practice has recently been formed, the CQS office encourages the applicant to provide a copy of the business plan provided to the applicant's PI insurers together with a business forecast for the next 12/24/36 months. The business forecast should include a forecast for the business as a whole with the residential conveyancing forecast shown as a percentage of that forecast.

All practices need to ensure that they have in place the required Core Practice Management Standards as set out in the application form. If the applicant finds when completing this part of the application form that they are responding 'no' or 'working towards' to a number of these Core Practice Management Standards, it is recommended that the applicant purchases the *Conveyancing Quality Scheme Toolkit* (available online from Law Society website) and/or contact Practice Advice Solicitors for advice as to how to set up, implement and embed these processes.

Applying as a newly formed practice should not be a daunting task and essentially, the CQS office needs to be assured that the financial standing, business model and effective management of the newly formed practice is in place. The more information an applicant is able to provide the better.

CQS's success and future

In March 2013, applications to the scheme were in excess of 2,900 with those accredited standing in excess of 2,300. Of those accredited, an additional 1,800 branch offices are in place making a total of 4,100 CQS 'outlets'. With the first practice to be accredited in February 2011, and CQS members now numbering over 2,300, a trusted community of firms has been quickly established.

Stakeholder buy-in to the scheme has been equally successful with Santander making CQS a prerequisite and others (such as Nationwide) confirming that anyone removed from their panel must have CQS before they will be reinstated. HSBC has made CQS members its second tier panel (which in effect means that any CQS member can act for HSBC), as have Yorkshire Bank and Clydesdale Bank.

Anecdotal evidence has suggested that being a member of the CQS has reduced PII premiums outside of the PII Scheme for CQS members that the Law Society facilitated and further, business for those that are CQS members has increased.

In 2013 further marketing is planned to raise awareness of the CQS with the public.

For more information

If you have any questions regarding the Conveyancing Quality Scheme, please contact the CQS office via email: cqs@lawsociety.org.uk or call: +44 (0)20 7316 5550.

Lexcel practice management standard

The Lexcel scheme is the only legally focused standard available to any size or type of legal practice in the world. There are currently over 1,500 accredited practices from sole practitioners to large law firms, and in-house legal departments in public to commercial sectors.

Written for solicitors, by solicitors, Lexcel provides practices with a framework to minimise exposure to risks and maximise operational efficiency using familiar terminology making it easy to understand and implement.

Consumers of legal services are becoming more empowered and have various options available to them when deciding which solicitor to use. Being Lexcel accredited provides assurance for your clients and prospective clients that they can expect to receive high quality and efficient services. It is thus a highly effective way to market your practice.

Benefits of Lexcel accreditation

Benefits of working towards and gaining accreditation include:

- increased operational efficiencies;
- improved competitive advantage;
- improved client care and customer service;
- more effective risk management;
- support to create a positive staff culture;
- the potential to reduce PII premiums.

The standard

The standard and scheme are reviewed regularly to ensure Lexcel remains relevant for legal practices. Lexcel v5 was launched on 31 October 2011 with additional requirements to assist practices to comply with outcomes-focused regulation. Practices should use Lexcel as a tool to create systems that will demonstrate compliance with the Code of Conduct 2011.

Management

Lexcel is managed by the Lexcel office of the Law Society. The Lexcel office administers and reviews all applications, oversees and manages the assessment process, promotes the scheme and develops the standard, scheme and all associated products. The Law Society is the only body with authority to award Lexcel accreditation.

The Lexcel Panel has overarching responsibility for the Lexcel standard and regularly provides advice to the Lexcel office on applications and the scheme's processes. The Panel comprises legal professionals from every size and type of practice.

Cost of accreditation

There are three main costs of applying for accreditation. These are:

1. *Resource cost* – how much it will take to work towards compliance using either internal resources or engaging with external experts.
2. *Application fees* – paid to the Law Society when submitting an application form and dependent on the size of your practice.
3. *Assessment fees* – paid to a Lexcel assessment body and dependent on the size of your practice.

The application process

The first action any practice should take is to complete the free Lexcel self-assessment checklist. This simple tool will help identify where you are compliant or non-compliant, as well as areas for improvement or development. For practices applying for the first time, the checklist gives you a good gauge as to how near to compliance the practice is.

There are key steps in the Lexcel process which must be adhered to when submitting an application and undertaking assessment. In brief, these are:

No.	Step	Duration/turnaround
1	Ensure the requirements are embedded	Must be in place at least 3 months
2	Submit Lexcel application form	Approval of application takes up to 4 weeks
3	If approval given, undertake an assessment	Duration depends on size of practice
4	Assessor submits report to the Lexcel office	Within 2 weeks of last on-site day
5	Complete any corrective action	Assessor will verify corrective action
6	Lexcel office reviews reports	4 week turnaround

Lexcel assessment bodies and assessors

Assessment bodies

Assessments are conducted by independent licensed assessment bodies. Lexcel assessors are employed by licensed assessment bodies and are all bound to ensure that the assessment is conducted in a compliant, confidential and independent manner. Assessment bodies are not allowed to provide consultancy and assessment services to the same practice. For details of the Lexcel assessment bodies, please visit: **www.lawsociety.org.uk/accreditation/lexcel/assessors-consultants**

Types of assessment

Initial assessments

All offices and practice areas must be included in the assessment. It is also mandatory that the assessor checks that all requirements of the Lexcel standard are being complied with.

Practices submitting an initial application must ensure the Lexcel requirements have been embedded for at least three months at the time of their assessment. This is to guarantee that there is sufficient evidence for the assessor to evaluate if all the requirements are correctly understood and embedded within the practice.

Annual maintenance visits (AMV) Year 1 and 2

During AMVs, the assessor must include all offices and practice areas in the assessment. All requirements in sections 6, 7 and 8 of the Lexcel standard must be assessed. In addition, any areas where non-compliances were found at the previous assessment must be reviewed.

For AMV1s, the assessor may tailor how sections 1 to 5 of standard are assessed to help the practice get the most benefit from the assessment. For example, if the practice has a very sound three-year business plan, the assessor may choose not to assess those sections of the Lexcel standard and focus on the areas that the practice was less strong on. For AMV2s, the assessor will need to assess any requirements from sections 1 to 5 that were not assessed during the AMV1.

The on-site duration for an AMV1 or AMV2 is approximately half that of an initial assessment.

Full re-assessment

On the third anniversary of the practice's initial award, a full re-assessment is required. This needs to take place in the month that they were initially awarded or the previous or following month, e.g. if the practice was awarded in June, then its AMV1 may take place in May, June or July.

During the full re-assessment the assessor must include all offices and practice areas in the assessment. All the requirements of the standard must be assessed.

The duration for a full re-assessment is the same as an initial assessment.

Joint assessments and passporting arrangements

There is a degree of synergy between Lexcel and IIP, ISO9001:2008 and the SQM. Practices who want multiple accreditation awards should consider undertaking simultaneous assessments. This typically reduces the overall duration of an assessment and, thus, reduces expenditure.

Practices can alternatively passport into Lexcel, particularly if they have undertaken another accreditation assessment within the past six months.

The overlaps and passporting grids can be found on the Lexcel website at: **www. lawsociety.org.uk/lexcel**

For more information

If you have any questions regarding the Lexcel scheme, please contact the Lexcel office via email: lexcel@lawsociety.org.uk or call: +44 (0)20 7320 5933.

APPENDIX B

Useful Law Society publications

Client Service for Law Firms, Heather Stewart

Conveyancing Quality Scheme Toolkit (2nd edition), The Law Society

Lexcel Business Continuity Planning Toolkit, The Law Society

Lexcel Client Care Toolkit (2nd edition), The Law Society

Lexcel Financial Management and Business Planning Toolkit, The Law Society

Lexcel Information Management Toolkit, The Law Society

Lexcel People Management Toolkit, The Law Society

Lexcel Risk Management Toolkit (2nd edition), The Law Society

Managing People in a Legal Business, edited by Jill Andrew

Marketing Legal Services (2nd edition), David Monk and Alastair Moyes

Practice Management Handbook (2nd edition), edited by Peter Scott

Profitability and Law Firm Management (2nd edition), Andrew Otterburn

Setting Up and Managing a Legal Practice (4th edition), Martin Smith

Special Report: Leadership for Law Firms, Patricia Wheatley Burt

Special Report: Social Media in the Legal Sector (forthcoming, 2013), Nathan Smith

Strategy for Law Firms, Nick Jarrett-Kerr

All books from Law Society Publishing can be ordered through good bookshops or direct from our distributors, Prolog, by telephone 0870 850 1422 or email lawsociety@prolog.uk.com. Please confirm the price before ordering.

For further information please visit our online bookshop at **www.lawsociety.org. uk/bookshop**